MznLnx

Missing Links Exam Preps

Exam Prep for

Investments

Sharpe, Alexander, Bailey, 6th Edition

The MznLnx Exam Prep is your link from the texbook and lecture to your exams.
The MznLnx Exam Preps are unauthorized and comprehensive reviews of your textbooks.

All material provided by MznLnx and Rico Publications (c) 2010
Textbook publishers and textbook authors do not particpate in or contribute to these reviews.

MznLnx

Rico
Publications

Exam Prep for Investments
6th Edition
Sharpe, Alexander, Bailey

Publisher: Raymond Houge
Assistant Editor: Michael Rouger
Text and Cover Designer: Lisa Buckner
Marketing Manager: Sara Swagger
Project Manager, Editorial Production: Jerry Emerson
Art Director: Vernon Lowerui

Product Manager: Dave Mason
Editorial Asitant: Rachel Guzmanji
Pedagogy: Debra Long
Cover Image: Jim Reed/Getty Images
Text and Cover Printer: City Printing, Inc.
Compositor: Media Mix, Inc.

(c) 2010 Rico Publications
ALL RIGHTS RESERVED. No part of this work
covered by the copyright may be reproduced or
used in any form or by an means--graphic, electronic,
or mechanical, including photocopying, recording,
taping, Web distribution, information storage, and
retrieval systems, or in any other manner--without the
written permission of the publisher.

Printed in the United States
ISBN:

For more information about our products, contact us at:
Dave.Mason@RicoPublications.com

For permission to use material from this text or
product, submit a request online to:
Dave.Mason@RicoPublications.com

Contents

CHAPTER 1
INTRODUCTION — 1

CHAPTER 2
BUYING AND SELLING SECURITIES — 11

CHAPTER 3
SECURITY MARKETS — 19

CHAPTER 4
EFFICIENT MARKETS, INVESTMENT VALUE, AND MARKET PRICE — 28

CHAPTER 5
THE VALUATION OF RISKLESS SECURITIES — 30

CHAPTER 6
THE PORTFOLIO SELECTION PROBLEM — 37

CHAPTER 7
PORTFOLIO ANALYSIS — 41

CHAPTER 8
RISKFREE BORROWING AND LENDING — 43

CHAPTER 9
THE CAPITAL ASSET PRICING MODEL — 45

CHAPTER 10
FACTOR MODELS — 52

CHAPTER 11
ARBITRAGE PRICING THEORY — 54

CHAPTER 12
TAXES AND INFLATION — 55

CHAPTER 13
FIXED-INCOME SECURITIES — 61

CHAPTER 14
BOND ANALYSIS — 73

CHAPTER 15
BOND PORTFOLIO MANAGEMENT — 80

CHAPTER 16
COMMON STOCKS — 87

CHAPTER 17
THE VALUATION OF COMMON STOCKS — 100

CHAPTER 18
EARNINGS — 105

CHAPTER 19
OPTIONS — 109

CHAPTER 20
FUTURES — 118

Contents (Cont.)

CHAPTER 21
   INVESTMENT COMPANIES   126
CHAPTER 22
   FINANCIAL ANALYSIS   131
CHAPTER 23
   INVESTMENT MANAGEMENT   139
CHAPTER 24
   PORTFOLIO PERFORMANCE EVALUATION   143
CHAPTER 25
   INTERNATIONAL INVESTING   149
ANSWER KEY   153

TO THE STUDENT

COMPREHENSIVE

The *MznLnx* Exam Prep series is designed to help you pass your exams. Editors at MznLnx review your textbooks and then prepare these practice exams to help you master the textbook material. Unlike study guides, workbooks, and practice tests provided by the texbook publisher and textbook authors, *MznLnx* gives you **all** of the material in each chapter in exam form, not just samples, so you can be sure to nail your exam.

MECHANICAL

The MznLnx Exam Prep series creates exams that will help you learn the subject matter as well as test you on your understanding. Each question is designed to help you master the concept. Just working through the exams, you gain an understanding of the subject--its a simple mechanical process that produces success.

INTEGRATED STUDY GUIDE AND REVIEW

MznLnx is not just a set of exams designed to test you, its also a comprehensive review of the subject content. Each exam question is also a review of the concept, making sure that you will get the answer correct without having to go to other sources of material. You learn as you go! Its the easiest way to pass an exam.

HUMOR

Studying can be tedious and dry. MznLnx's instructional design includes moderate humor within the exam questions on occassion, to break the tedium and revitalize the brain

Chapter 1. INTRODUCTION

1. In lending agreements, _____ is a borrower's pledge of specific property to a lender, to secure repayment of a loan. The _____ serves as protection for a lender against a borrower's risk of default - that is, a borrower failing to pay the principal and interest under the terms of a loan obligation. If a borrower does default on a loan (due to insolvency or other event), that borrower forfeits (gives up) the property pledged as _____ *ollateral* - and the lender then becomes the owner of the _____.

   a. Nominal value
   b. Refinancing risk
   c. Collateral
   d. Future-oriented

2. A _____ is defined as a certificate of agreement of loans which is given under the company's stamp and carries an undertaking that the _____ holder will get a fixed return (fixed on the basis of interest rates) and the principal amount whenever the _____ matures.

   In finance, a _____ is a long-term debt instrument used by governments and large companies to obtain funds. It is defined as 'a debt secured only by the debtor's earning power, not by a lien on any specific asset.' It is similar to a bond except the securitization conditions are different.

   a. Partial Payment
   b. Collateral Management
   c. Debenture
   d. Collection agency

3. The _____ is that part of the capital markets that deals with the issuance of new securities. Companies, governments or public sector institutions can obtain funding through the sale of a new stock or bond issue. This is typically done through a syndicate of securities dealers.

   a. Sector rotation
   b. Peer group analysis
   c. Volatility clustering
   d. Primary market

4. A _____, referred to as a note payable in accounting, is a contract where one party (the maker or issuer) makes an unconditional promise in writing to pay a sum of money to the other (the payee), either at a fixed or determinable future time or on demand of the payee, under specific terms. They differ from IOUs in that they contain a specific promise to pay, rather than simply acknowledging that a debt exists.

   The terms of a note typically include the principal amount, the interest rate if any, and the maturity date.

   a. Promissory note
   b. Financial plan
   c. Credit repair software
   d. Title loan

5. The _____ is the financial market where previously issued securities and financial instruments such as stock, bonds, options, and futures are bought and sold. The term '_____' is also used refer to the market for any used goods or assets, or an alternative use for an existing product or asset where the customer base is the second market

   With primary issuances of securities or financial instruments, or the primary market, investors purchase these securities directly from issuers such as corporations issuing shares in an IPO or private placement, or directly from the federal government in the case of treasuries.

   a. Financial market
   b. Delta neutral
   c. Secondary market
   d. Performance attribution

Chapter 1. INTRODUCTION

6. A _____ is a fungible, negotiable instrument representing financial value. They are broadly categorized into debt securities (such as banknotes, bonds and debentures), and equity securities; e.g., common stocks. The company or other entity issuing the _____ is called the issuer.
   a. Tracking stock
   b. Book entry
   c. Security
   d. Securities lending

7. In finance, a _____ is a debt security, in which the authorized issuer owes the holders a debt and, depending on the terms of the _____, is obliged to pay interest (the coupon) and/or to repay the principal at a later date, termed maturity.

   Thus a _____ is a loan: the issuer is the borrower, the _____ holder is the lender, and the coupon is the interest. _____s provide the borrower with external funds to finance long-term investments, or, in the case of government _____s, to finance current expenditure.

   a. Catastrophe bonds
   b. Convertible bond
   c. Puttable bond
   d. Bond

8. The institution most often referenced by the word '_____' is a public or publicly traded _____, the shares of which are traded on a public stock exchange (e.g., the New York Stock Exchange or Nasdaq in the United States) where shares of stock of _____s are bought and sold by and to the general public. Most of the largest businesses in the world are publicly traded _____s. However, the majority of _____s are said to be closely held, privately held or close _____s, meaning that no ready market exists for the trading of shares.
   a. Corporation
   b. Federal Home Loan Mortgage Corporation
   c. Depository Trust Company
   d. Protect

9. The coupon or _____ of a bond is the amount of interest paid per year expressed as a percentage of the face value of the bond.

   For example if you hold $10,000 nominal of a bond described as a 4.5% loan stock, you will receive $450 in interest each year (probably in two installments of $225 each.)

   Not all bonds have coupons.

   a. Zero-coupon bond
   b. Revenue bonds
   c. Puttable bond
   d. Coupon rate

10. A _____ is an international bond that is denominated in a currency not native to the country where it is issued. It can be categorised according to the currency in which it is issued. London is one of the centers of the _____ market, but _____s may be traded throughout the world - for example in Singapore or Tokyo.
    a. Economic entity
    b. Interest rate option
    c. Education production function
    d. Eurobond

11. A _____ is a bond issued by a national government denominated in the country's own currency. Bonds issued by national governments in foreign currencies are normally referred to as sovereign bonds. The first ever _____ was issued by the British government in 1693 to raise money to fund a war against France.

Chapter 1. INTRODUCTION

    a. Municipal bond
    c. Collateralized debt obligations
    b. Zero-coupon bond
    d. Government bond

12. In economic models, the _____ time frame assumes no fixed factors of production. Firms can enter or leave the marketplace, and the cost (and availability) of land, labor, raw materials, and capital goods can be assumed to vary. In contrast, in the short-run time frame, certain factors are assumed to be fixed, because there is not sufficient time for them to change.
    a. Long-run
    c. Short-run
    b. 4-4-5 Calendar
    d. 529 plan

13. _____ is a life of security. It may also refer to the final payment date of a loan or other financial instrument, at which point all remaining interest and principal is due to be paid.

1, 3, 6 months _____ band can be calculated by using 30-day per month periods.

    a. False billing
    c. Primary market
    b. Maturity
    d. Replacement cost

14. In finance, _____, also known as return on investment is the ratio of money gained or lost on an investment relative to the amount of money invested. The amount of money gained or lost may be referred to as interest, profit/loss, gain/loss, or net income/loss. The money invested may be referred to as the asset, capital, principal, or the cost basis of the investment.
    a. Compposiition of Creditors
    c. Stock or scrip dividends
    b. Rate of return
    d. Doctrine of the Proper Law

15. _____ mature in one year or less. Like zero-coupon bonds, they do not pay interest prior to maturity; instead they are sold at a discount of the par value to create a positive yield to maturity. Many regard _____ as the least risky investment available to U.S. investors.
    a. 4-4-5 Calendar
    c. Treasury securities
    b. Treasury bills
    d. Treasury Inflation Protected Securities

16. _____ are government bonds issued by the United States Department of the Treasury through the Bureau of the Public Debt. They are the debt financing instruments of the U.S. Federal government, and they are often referred to simply as Treasuries or Treasurys. There are four types of marketable _____: Treasury bills, Treasury notes, Treasury bonds, and Treasury Inflation Protected Securities (TIPS.)
    a. 4-4-5 Calendar
    c. Treasury securities
    b. Treasury Inflation-Protected Securities
    d. Treasury Inflation Protected Securities

17. _____ refers to any type of investment that yields a regular (or fixed) return.

For example, if you lend money to a borrower and the borrower has to pay interest once a month, you have been issued a fixed-income security. When a company does this, it is often called a bond or corporate bank debt (although preferred stock is also sometimes considered to be _____).

a. Bond market
b. 4-4-5 Calendar
c. 529 plan
d. Fixed income

18. In economics, _____ is a rise in the general level of prices of goods and services in an economy over a period of time. The term '_____' once referred to increases in the money supply (monetary _____); however, economic debates about the relationship between money supply and price levels have led to its primary use today in describing price _____. _____ can also be described as a decline in the real value of money--a loss of purchasing power in the medium of exchange which is also the monetary unit of account.
   a. AAB
   b. A Random Walk Down Wall Street
   c. ABN Amro
   d. Inflation

19. A _____ is a bond issued by a corporation. The term is usually applied to longer-term debt instruments, generally with a maturity date falling at least a year after their issue date. (The term 'commercial paper' is sometimes used for instruments with a shorter maturity.)
   a. Serial bond
   b. Brady bonds
   c. Corporate bond
   d. Government bond

20. _____ are organizations which pool large sums of money and invest those sums in companies. They include banks, insurance companies, retirement or pension funds, hedge funds and mutual funds. Their role in the economy is to act as highly specialized investors on behalf of others.
   a. A Random Walk Down Wall Street
   b. AAB
   c. Institutional investors
   d. ABN Amro

21. _____ consists of the sale of goods or merchandise from a fixed location, such as a department store, boutique or kiosk in small or individual lots for direct consumption by the purchaser. _____ may include subordinated services, such as delivery. Purchasers may be individuals or businesses.
   a. Retailing
   b. 4-4-5 Calendar
   c. 7-Eleven
   d. 529 plan

22. A _____ is a financial debt vehicle that was first created in June 1983 by investment banks Salomon Brothers and First Boston for Freddie Mac. (The First Boston team was led by Dexter Senft.) Legally, a _____ is a special purpose entity that is wholly separate from the institution(s) that create it.
   a. Tranche
   b. 4-4-5 Calendar
   c. Yield curve spread
   d. Collateralized mortgage obligation

23. _____ is a form of corporation equity ownership represented in the securities. It is dangerous in comparison to preferred shares and some other investment options, in that in the event of bankruptcy, _____ investors receive their funds after preferred stockholders, bondholders, creditors, etc. On the other hand, common shares on average perform better than preferred shares or bonds over time.
   a. Stock split
   b. Stop-limit order
   c. Stock market bubble
   d. Common stock

24. In finance, a _____ is a standardized contract, to buy or sell a specified commodity of standardized quality at a certain date in the future, at a market determined price (the futures price.)

Chapter 1. INTRODUCTION

The price is determined by the instantaneous equilibrium between the forces of supply and demand among competing buy and sell orders on the exchange at the time of the purchase or sale of the contract.

In many cases, the items may be such non-traditional 'commodities' as foreign currencies, commercial or government paper [e.g., bonds], or 'baskets' of corporate equity ['stock indices'] or other financial instruments.

a. Financial future
b. Futures contract
c. Heston model
d. Repurchase agreement

25. In business and finance, a _____ (also referred to as equity _____) of stock means a _____ of ownership in a corporation (company.) In the plural, stocks is often used as a synonym for _____s especially in the United States, but it is less commonly used that way outside of North America.

In the United Kingdom, South Africa, and Australia, stock can also refer to completely different financial instruments such as government bonds or, less commonly, to all kinds of marketable securities.

a. Bucket shop
b. Margin
c. Procter ' Gamble
d. Share

26. _____ in finance is a risk management technique, related to hedging, that mixes a wide variety of investments within a portfolio. Because the fluctuations of a single security have less impact on a diverse portfolio, _____ minimizes the risk from any one investment.

A simple example of _____ is the following: On a particular island the entire economy consists of two companies: one that sells umbrellas and another that sells sunscreen.

a. 7-Eleven
b. Diversification
c. 4-4-5 Calendar
d. 529 plan

27. A _____ is a situation that involves losing one quality or aspect of something in return for gaining another quality or aspect. It implies a decision to be made with full comprehension of both the upside and downside of a particular choice.

In economics the term is expressed as opportunity cost, referring the most preferred alternative given up.

a. Break-even point
b. Trade-off
c. Capital outflow
d. Total revenue

28. The _____ is the market for securities, where companies and governments can raise longterm funds. The _____ includes the stock market and the bond market. Financial regulators, such as the U.S. Securities and Exchange Commission, oversee the _____s in their designated countries to ensure that investors are protected against fraud.

a. Spot rate
b. Delta neutral
c. Forward market
d. Capital market

29. A _____ is an institution, firm or individual who mediates between two or more parties in a financial context. Typically the first party is a provider of a product or service and the second party is a consumer or customer.

Chapter 1. INTRODUCTION

In the U.S., a _____ is typically an institution that facilitates the channelling of funds between lenders and borrowers indirectly.

   a. Savings and loan association   b. Mutual fund
   c. Financial intermediary   d. Net asset value

30. _____, is when a company issues common stock or shares to the public for the first time. They are often issued by smaller, younger companies seeking capital to expand, but can also be done by large privately-owned companies looking to become publicly traded.

In an _____ the issuer may obtain the assistance of an underwriting firm, which helps it determine what type of security to issue (common or preferred), best offering price and time to bring it to market.

   a. Initial public offering   b. Insolvency
   c. Interest   d. Asian Financial Crisis

31. In finance, the _____ is the global financial market for short-term borrowing and lending. It provides short-term liquidity funding for the global financial system. The _____ is where short-term obligations such as Treasury bills, commercial paper and bankers' acceptances are bought and sold.
   a. Money market   b. Debt-for-equity swap
   c. Cramdown   d. Consumer debt

32. A _____, securities exchange or (in Europe) bourse is a corporation or mutual organization which provides 'trading' facilities for stock brokers and traders, to trade stocks and other securities. _____s also provide facilities for the issue and redemption of securities as well as other financial instruments and capital events including the payment of income and dividends. The securities traded on a _____ include: shares issued by companies, unit trusts and other pooled investment products and bonds.
   a. 4-4-5 Calendar   b. Stock Exchange
   c. 7-Eleven   d. 529 plan

33. A _____ is a measure of the average price of consumer goods and services purchased by households. The _____ can be used to index (i.e., adjust for the effects of inflation) wages, salaries, pensions, or regulated or contracted prices. The _____ is, along with the population census and the National Income and Product Accounts, one of the most closely watched national economic statistics.
   a. 529 plan   b. Divisia index
   c. Consumer price index   d. 4-4-5 Calendar

34. _____ is the provision of resources (such as granting a loan) by one party to another party where that second party does not reimburse the first party immediately, thereby generating a debt, and instead arranges either to repay or return those resources (or material(s) of equal value) at a later date. The first party is called a creditor, also known as a lender, while the second party is called a debtor, also known as a borrower.

Movements of financial capital are normally dependent on either _____ or equity transfers.

Chapter 1. INTRODUCTION

a. Clearing house
b. Credit
c. Comparable
d. Warrant

35. A _____ is a cooperative financial institution that is owned and controlled by its members, and operated for the purpose of promoting thrift, providing credit at reasonable rates, and providing other financial services to its members. Many _____s exist to further community development or sustainable international development on a local level. Worldwide, _____ systems vary significantly in terms of total system assets and average institution asset size since _____s exist in a wide range of sizes, ranging from volunteer operations with a handful of members to institutions with several billion dollars in assets and hundreds of thousands of members.

a. Credit union
b. Corporate credit union
c. Fi-linx
d. Credit Union Service Organization

36. An _____ is any government regulation or law that encourages or discourages foreign investment in the local economy, e.g. currency exchange limits.

As globalization integrates the economies of neighboring and of trading states, they are typically forced to trade off such rules as part of a common tax, tariff and trade regime, e.g. as defined by a free trade pact. _____ favoring local investors over global ones is typically discouraged in such pacts, and the idea of a separate _____ rapidly becomes a fiction or fantasy, as real decisions reflect the real need for nations to compete for investment, even from their own local investors.

a. AAB
b. ABN Amro
c. A Random Walk Down Wall Street
d. Investment policy

37. A _____ is a professionally managed type of collective investment scheme that pools money from many investors and invests it in stocks, bonds, short-term money market instruments, and/or other securities. The _____ will have a fund manager that trades the pooled money on a regular basis. Currently, the worldwide value of all _____s totals more than $26 trillion.

Since 1940, there have been three basic types of investment companies in the United States: open-end funds, also known in the US as _____s; unit investment trusts (UITs); and closed-end funds.

a. Net asset value
b. Mutual fund
c. Trust company
d. Financial intermediary

38. A _____ is a pool of assets forming an independent legal entity that are bought with the contributions to a pension plan for the exclusive purpose of financing pension plan benefits.

_____s are important shareholders of listed and private companies. They are especially important to the stock market where large institutional investors like the Ontario Teachers' Pension Plan dominate.

a. Leveraged buyout
b. Pension fund
c. Leverage
d. Limited liability company

Chapter 1. INTRODUCTION

39. A _____ is a normalized average (typically a weighted average) of prices for a given class of goods or services in a given region, during a given interval of time. It is a statistic designed to help to compare how these prices, taken as a whole, differ between time periods or geographical locations.

   a. Transfer pricing
   b. Price discrimination
   c. Discounts and allowances
   d. Price Index

40. A _____ is a financial institution that specializes in accepting savings deposits and making mortgage and other loans. The S'L or thrift term is mainly used in the United States; similar institutions in the United Kingdom, Ireland and some Commonwealth countries include building societies and trustee savings banks.

   They are often mutually held, meaning that the depositors and borrowers are members with voting rights, and have the ability to direct the financial and managerial goals of the organization, not unlike the poliyholders of a mutual insurance company.

   a. Net asset value
   b. Mutual fund
   c. Person-to-person lending
   d. Savings and loan association

41. _____ of a business involves analyzing its financial statements and health, its management and competitive advantages, and its competitors and markets. The term is used to distinguish such analysis from other types of investment analysis, such as quantitative analysis and technical analysis.

   _____ is performed on historical and present data, but with the goal of making financial forecasts.

   a. Growth stocks
   b. 4-4-5 Calendar
   c. Stock valuation
   d. Fundamental analysis

42. _____, authored by professors Benjamin Graham and David Dodd of Columbia Business School, laid the intellectual foundation for what would later be called value investing. The work was first published in 1934, following unprecedented losses on Wall Street. In summing up lessons learned, Graham and Dodd chided Wall Street for its myopic focus on a company's reported earnings per share, and were particularly harsh on the favored 'earnings trends.' They encouraged investors to take an entirely different approach by gauging the rough value of the operating business that lay behind the security.

   a. Stock valuation
   b. Security analysis
   c. Growth stocks
   d. 4-4-5 Calendar

43. _____ is a security analysis discipline for forecasting the future direction of prices through the study of past market data, primarily price and volume. In its purest form, _____ considers only the actual price and volume behavior of the market or instrument. Technical analysts may employ models and trading rules based on price and volume transformations, such as the relative strength index, moving averages, regressions, inter-market and intra-market price correlations, cycles or, classically, through recognition of chart patterns.

   a. Point and figure
   b. Support and resistance
   c. Technical analysis
   d. Dow theory

Chapter 1. INTRODUCTION

44. _____ refers to a portfolio management strategy where the manager makes specific investments with the goal of outperforming an investment benchmark index. Investors or mutual funds that do not aspire to create a return in excess of a benchmark index will often invest in an index fund that replicates as closely as possible the investment weighting and returns of that index; this is called passive management. _____ is the opposite of passive management, because in passive management the manager does not seek to outperform the benchmark index.

   a. A Random Walk Down Wall Street
   b. AAB
   c. ABN Amro
   d. Active management

45. An _____ is a document, generally between an investor and the assisting investment manager, recording the agreements the two parties come to with regards to issues relating to how the investor's money is to be managed. In other cases, an _____ may also be created by an investment committee to help establish and record its own policies in order to assist in future decision-making or to help maintain consistency of its policies by future committee members or to clarify expectations for prospective money managers who may be hired by the committee.

   The presence of an _____ helps to clearly communicate to all relevant parties the procedures, investment philosophy, guidelines and constraints to be adhered to by the parties.

   a. Investment Policy Statement
   b. A Random Walk Down Wall Street
   c. ABN Amro
   d. AAB

46. A _____ is a brief written statement of the purpose of a company or organization. Ideally, a _____ guides the actions of the organization, spells out its overall goal, provides a sense of direction, and guides decision making for all levels of management.

   _____s often contain the following:

   - Purpose and aim of the organization
   - The organization's primary stakeholders: clients, stockholders, etc.
   - Responsibilities of the organization toward these stakeholders
   - Products and services offered

   In developing a _____:

   - Encourage as much input as feasible from employees, volunteers, and other stakeholders
   - Publicize it broadly

   The _____ can be used to resolve differences between business stakeholders. Stakeholders include: employees including managers and executives, stockholders, board of directors, customers, suppliers, distributors, creditors, governments (local, state, federal, etc.), unions, competitors, NGO's, and the general public.

   a. Mission statement
   b. 529 plan
   c. 4-4-5 Calendar
   d. 7-Eleven

47. In economics and finance, _____ is the practice of taking advantage of a price differential between two or more markets: striking a combination of matching deals that capitalize upon the imbalance, the profit being the difference between the market prices. When used by academics, an _____ is a transaction that involves no negative cash flow at any probabilistic or temporal state and a positive cash flow in at least one state; in simple terms, a risk-free profit.
   a. Efficient-market hypothesis
   b. Issuer
   c. Initial margin
   d. Arbitrage

48. In business and accounting, _____s are everything of value that is owned by a person or company. The balance sheet of a firm records the monetary value of the _____s owned by the firm. The two major _____ classes are tangible _____s and intangible _____s.
   a. Accounts payable
   b. Income
   c. Asset
   d. EBITDA

49. _____ is an international professional designation offered by the _____ Institute (formerly known as AIMR) to financial analysts who complete a series of three examinations. In order to become a '_____ Charterholder' candidates must pass all three six-hour exams, possess a bachelor's degree (or equivalent, as assessed by the _____ institute) and have 48 months of work experience in an investment decision-making position. _____ charterholders are also obligated to adhere to a strict Code of Ethics and Standards governing their professional conduct.
   a. 4-4-5 Calendar
   b. 529 plan
   c. 7-Eleven
   d. Chartered Financial Analyst

50. A _____, securities analyst, research analyst, equity analyst, or investment analyst is a person who performs financial analysis for external or internal clients as a core part of the job.

An analyst studies companies and other entities to arrive at the estimate of their financial value. It is normally done by analyzing financial reports, aided by follow-up interviews with company representatives and industry experts.

   a. Purchasing manager
   b. Portfolio manager
   c. Stockbroker
   d. Financial Analyst

Chapter 2. BUYING AND SELLING SECURITIES

1. _____, in bookkeeping, refers to assets, liabilities, income, and expenses recorded on individual pages of the so called book of final entry or ledger. Changes in _____ value are made by chronologically posting debit (DR) and credit (CR) entries to its page. Examples of _____s are cash, _____s receivable, mortgages, loans, land and buildings, common stock, sales, services provided, wages, and payroll overhead.
   - a. Accretion
   - b. Alpha
   - c. Option
   - d. Account

2. A '_____' is a 'Charge' that is paid to obtain the right to delay a payment. Essentially, the payer purchases the right to make a given payment in the future instead of in the Present. The '_____', or 'Charge' that must be paid to delay the payment, is simply the difference between what the payment amount would be if it were paid in the present and what the payment amount would be paid if it were paid in the future.
   - a. Risk aversion
   - b. Risk modeling
   - c. Discount
   - d. Value at risk

3. A _____ is a fungible, negotiable instrument representing financial value. They are broadly categorized into debt securities (such as banknotes, bonds and debentures), and equity securities; e.g., common stocks. The company or other entity issuing the _____ is called the issuer.
   - a. Book entry
   - b. Tracking stock
   - c. Securities lending
   - d. Security

4. The _____ (NYSE: FNM), commonly known as Fannie Mae, is a stockholder-owned corporation chartered by Congress in 1968 as a government sponsored enterprise (GSE), but founded in 1938 during the Great Depression. The corporation's purpose is to purchase and securitize mortgages in order to ensure that funds are consistently available to the institutions that lend money to home buyers.

On September 7, 2008, James Lockhart, director of the Federal Housing Finance Agency (FHFA), announced that Fannie Mae and Freddie Mac were being placed into conservatorship of the FHFA.

   - a. SPDR
   - b. Federal National Mortgage Association
   - c. General partnership
   - d. The Depository Trust ' Clearing Corporation

5. A _____ is an order to buy a security at no more (or sell at no less) than a specific price. This gives the customer some control over the price at which the trade is executed, but may prevent the order from being executed ('filled'.)

A buy _____ can only be executed by the broker at the limit price or lower.

   - a. Common stock
   - b. Block premium
   - c. Commercial mortgage-backed securities
   - d. Limit order

6. A _____ is a buy or sell order to be executed by the broker immediately at current market prices. As long as there are willing sellers and buyers, _____s are filled.

A _____ is the simplest of the order types.

   - a. Trading curb
   - b. Stockholder
   - c. Block premium
   - d. Market order

Chapter 2. BUYING AND SELLING SECURITIES

7. A _____ is an order to buy (or sell) a security once the price of the security has climbed above (or dropped below) a specified stop price. When the specified stop price is reached, the _____ is entered as a market order (no limit.)

With a _____, the customer does not have to actively monitor how a stock is performing.

   a. Stock split
   c. Share price
   b. Wash sale
   d. Stop order

8. In finance, the _____ is used to determine a theoretically appropriate required rate of return of an asset, if that asset is to be added to an already well-diversified portfolio, given that asset's non-diversifiable risk. The model takes into account the asset's sensitivity to non-diversifiable risk (also known as systemic risk or market risk), often represented by the quantity beta (β) in the financial industry, as well as the expected return of the market and the expected return of a theoretical risk-free asset.

The model was introduced by Jack Treynor (1961, 1962), William Sharpe (1964), John Lintner (1965a,b) and Jan Mossin (1966) independently, building on the earlier work of Harry Markowitz on diversification and modern portfolio theory.

   a. Capital asset pricing model
   c. Cox-Ingersoll-Ross model
   b. Random walk hypothesis
   d. Hull-White model

9. The term _____ has three unrelated technical definitions, and is also used in a variety of non-technical ways.

   - In financial economics, it refers to any asset used to make money, as opposed to assets used for personal enjoyment or consumption. This is an important distinction because two people can disagree sharply about the value of personal assets, one person might think a sports car is more valuable than a pickup truck, another person might have the opposite taste. But if an asset is held for the purpose of making money, taste has nothing to do with it, only differences of opinion about how much money the asset will produce. With the further assumption that people agree on the probability distribution of future cash flows, it is possible to have an objective _____ pricing model. Even without the assumption of agreement, it is possible to set rational limits on _____ value.
   - In governmental accounting, it is defined as any asset used in operations with an initial useful life extending beyond one reporting period. Generally, government managers have a 'stewardship' duty to maintain _____s under their control. See International Public Sector Accounting Standards for details.
   - In US tax accounting, it is defined as any property other than a list of exceptions. The main exceptions are anything held for sale, and any real estate or depreciable property used in business. Almost everything you own and use for personal purposes, pleasure or investment is a _____. If something is a _____ for tax purposes, gains or losses on sale or disposition are capital gains or capital losses. For individuals, however, capital losses on property held for personal use are generally not deductible. See the IRS publication Tax Facts about Capital Gains and Losses for details.

A well-known financial accounting textbook advises that the term be avoided except in tax accounting because it is used in so many different senses, not all of them well-defined. For example it is often used as a synonym for fixed assets or for investments in securities.

A common non-technical usage occurs when people ask that employees or the environment or something else be treated as a _____.

a. Solvency
b. Settlement date
c. Political risk
d. Capital asset

10. Generally, in English and American law, a contract of mortgage or pledge as collateral for a debt in which the subject matter is not delivered into the possession of the pledgee or pawnee. The arrangement is common with modern mortgages - the borrower retains legal ownership of the property but provides the lender with a lien over the property until the debt is paid off.

_____ and re-_____, respectively, are commonly used to describe the means by which securities brokers and dealers first extend credit on margin to their customers using pledged securities as collateral, and then pledge the client-owned securities held in the client's margin account as collateral for the brokerage's bank loan.

a. Hypothecation
b. 4-4-5 Calendar
c. 7-Eleven
d. 529 plan

11. An _____ is a retirement plan account that provides some tax advantages for retirement savings in the United States.

a. A Random Walk Down Wall Street
b. Individual Retirement Arrangement
c. ABN Amro
d. AAB

12. A _____ is the price set by a monopolist to discourage economic entry into a market, and is illegal in many countries. The _____ is the price that the entrant would face upon entering as long as the incumbent firm did not decrease output. The _____ is often lower than the average cost of production or just low enough to make entering not profitable. The quantity produced by the incumbent firm to act as a deterrent to entry is usually larger than would be optimal for a monopolist, but might still produce higher economic profits than would be earned under perfect competition. The problem with limit pricing as strategic behavior is that once the entrant has entered the market, the quantity used as a threat to deter entry is no longer the incumbent firm's best response.

a. Limit price
b. 4-4-5 Calendar
c. 7-Eleven
d. 529 plan

13. In finance, a _____ is collateral that the holder of a position in securities, options, or futures contracts has to deposit to cover the credit risk of his counterparty (most often his broker.) This risk can arise if the holder has done any of the following:

- borrowed cash from the counterparty to buy securities or options,
- sold securities or options short, or
- entered into a futures contract.

The collateral can be in the form of cash or securities, and it is deposited in a _____ account. On U.S. futures exchanges, '_____' was formally called performance bond.

_____ buying is buying securities with cash borrowed from a broker, using other securities as collateral.

Chapter 2. BUYING AND SELLING SECURITIES

a. Share
c. Credit
b. Procter ' Gamble
d. Margin

14. The collateral can be in the form of cash or securities, and it is deposited in a _____. On U.S. futures exchanges, 'margin' was formally called performance bond.

Margin buying is buying securities with cash borrowed from a broker, using other securities as collateral.

a. Risk-neutral measure
c. Margin account
b. Dollar roll
d. Forward contract

15. A _____ combines the features of a stop order and a limit order. Once the stop price is reached, the _____ becomes a limit order to buy (or to sell) at no more (or less) than a specified price. As with all limit orders, a _____ doesn't get filled if the security's price never reaches the specified limit price.

a. Stop price
c. Box spread
b. Stop-limit order
d. Wash sale

16. A _____ is the price in stop order that triggers creation of market order.

In the case of a Sell on Stop order, when the market reaches or falls below the _____ a market sell order will be triggered. For Buy on Stop orders, the _____ triggers the creation of a market buy order when the market price of the stock rises to or above the _____.

a. Whisper numbers
c. Stop price
b. Stockholder
d. Box spread

17. In business and accounting, _____s are everything of value that is owned by a person or company. The balance sheet of a firm records the monetary value of the _____s owned by the firm. The two major _____ classes are tangible _____s and intangible _____s.

a. Asset
c. Income
b. EBITDA
d. Accounts payable

18. In finance, _____ is the process of estimating the potential market value of a financial asset or liability. they can be done on assets (for example, investments in marketable securities such as stocks, options, business enterprises, or intangible assets such as patents and trademarks) or on liabilities (e.g., Bonds issued by a company.) _____s are required in many contexts including investment analysis, capital budgeting, merger and acquisition transactions, financial reporting, taxable events to determine the proper tax liability, and in litigation.

a. Share
c. Margin
b. Valuation
d. Procter ' Gamble

19. _____ refers to a business or organization attempting to acquire goods or services to accomplish the goals of the enterprise. Though there are several organizations that attempt to set standards in the _____ process, processes can vary greatly between organizations. Typically the word '_____' is not used interchangeably with the word 'procurement', since procurement typically includes Expediting, Supplier Quality, and Traffic and Logistics (T'L) in addition to _____.

Chapter 2. BUYING AND SELLING SECURITIES

a. 4-4-5 Calendar
c. 7-Eleven
b. 529 plan
d. Purchasing

20. The _____ requirement is the amount required to be collateralized in order to open a position. Thereafter, the amount required to be kept in collateral until the position is closed is the maintenance requirement. The maintenance requirement is the minimum amount to be collateralized in order to keep an open position.
   a. Issuer
   b. Arbitrage
   c. Efficient-market hypothesis
   d. Initial margin

21. The _____ is the amount required to be collateralized in order to open a position. Thereafter, the amount required to be kept in collateral until the position is closed is the maintenance requirement. The maintenance requirement is the minimum amount to be collateralized in order to keep an open position.
   a. AAB
   b. ABN Amro
   c. A Random Walk Down Wall Street
   d. Initial margin requirement

22. The variation margin or _____ is not collateral, but a daily offsetting of profits and losses. Futures are marked-to-market every day, so the current price is compared to the previous day's price. The profit or loss on the day of a position is then paid to or debited from the holder by the futures exchange.
   a. Delivery month
   b. Total return swap
   c. SPI 200 futures contract
   d. Maintenance margin

23. The _____, sometimes called the maintenance margin requirement, is the ratio set for:

   - (Stock Equity - Leveraged Dollars) to Stock Equity

   - Stock Equity being the stock price * no. of stocks bought and Leveraged Dollars being the amount borrowed in the margin account.

   - E.g. An investor bought 1000 shares of ABC company each priced at $50. If the initial margin requirement were 60%:

   - Stock Equity: $50 * 1000 = $50,000

   - Leveraged Dollars or amount borrowed: ($50 * 1000)* (1-60%) = $20,000

So the maintenance margin requirement uses the above variables to form a ratio that investors have to abide by in order to keep the account active.

Chapter 2. BUYING AND SELLING SECURITIES

The point is, let's say the maintenance margin requirement is reduced from 60% to 25% - At what price would the investor be getting a margin call? Let P be the price, so 1000P in our case is the Stock Equity.

- (Stock Equity - Leveraged Dollars) divided by Stock Equity = 25%

- (1000P - $20,000)/1000P = 0.25

- (1000P - $20,000) = 250P

- P = $26.67

So if the stock price drops from $50 to $26.67, investors will be called to add additional funds to the account to make up for the loss in stock equity.

Margin requirements are reduced for positions that offset each other.

a. 7-Eleven
b. 4-4-5 Calendar
c. Minimum margin requirement
d. 529 plan

24. In finance, _____ (or gearing) is borrowing money to supplement existing funds for investment in such a way that the potential positive or negative outcome is magnified and/or enhanced. It generally refers to using borrowed funds, or debt, so as to attempt to increase the returns to equity. Deleveraging is the action of reducing borrowings.
a. Pension fund
b. Leverage
c. Financial endowment
d. Limited partnership

25. In finance, _____, also known as return on investment is the ratio of money gained or lost on an investment relative to the amount of money invested. The amount of money gained or lost may be referred to as interest, profit/loss, gain/loss, or net income/loss. The money invested may be referred to as the asset, capital, principal, or the cost basis of the investment.
a. Doctrine of the Proper Law
b. Stock or scrip dividends
c. Composiition of Creditors
d. Rate of return

26. In finance, _____ or 'shorting' is the practice of selling a financial instrument that the seller does not own at the time of the sale. _____ is done with intent of later purchasing the financial instrument at a lower price. Short-sellers attempt to profit from an expected decline in the price of a financial instrument.
a. 529 plan
b. Short ratio
c. 4-4-5 Calendar
d. Short selling

27. A _____ is a payment made by a corporation to its shareholder members. When a corporation earns a profit or surplus, that money can be put to two uses: it can either be re-invested in the business (called retained earnings), or it can be paid to the shareholders as a _____. Many corporations retain a portion of their earnings and pay the remainder as a _____.
a. Dividend yield
b. Dividend puzzle
c. Special dividend
d. Dividend

Chapter 2. BUYING AND SELLING SECURITIES

28. In finance, a _____ is a standardized contract, to buy or sell a specified commodity of standardized quality at a certain date in the future, at a market determined price (the futures price.)

The price is determined by the instantaneous equilibrium between the forces of supply and demand among competing buy and sell orders on the exchange at the time of the purchase or sale of the contract.

In many cases, the items may be such non-traditional 'commodities' as foreign currencies, commercial or government paper [e.g., bonds], or 'baskets' of corporate equity ['stock indices'] or other financial instruments.

- a. Futures contract
- b. Heston model
- c. Repurchase agreement
- d. Financial future

29. In finance, _____ or stock lending refers to the lending of securities by one party to another. The terms of the loan will be governed by a '_____ Agreement', which, under U.S. law, requires that the borrower provides the lender with collateral, in the form of cash, government securities, or a Letter of Credit of value equal to or greater than the loaned securities. As payment for the loan, the parties negotiate a fee, quoted as an annualized percentage of the value of the loaned securities.
- a. Tracking stock
- b. Securities lending
- c. Marketable
- d. Book entry

30. In finance, a _____ is a position established in one market in an attempt to offset exposure to the price risk of an equal but opposite obligation or position in another market -- usually, but not always, in the context of one's commercial activity. Hedging is a strategy designed to minimize exposure to such business risks as a sharp contraction in demand for one's inventory, while still allowing the business to profit from producing and maintaining that inventory. A typical hedger might be a farmer with 2000 acres of unharvested wheat in the ground, who would rather tend his crop without the distraction of uncertain prices.
- a. 4-4-5 Calendar
- b. 529 plan
- c. 7-Eleven
- d. Hedge

31. A _____ is a private investment fund open to a limited range of investors that is permitted by regulators to undertake a wider range of activities than other investment funds and also pays a performance fee to its investment manager. Each fund will have its own strategy which determines the type of investments and the methods of investment it undertakes. _____s as a class invest in a broad range of investments extending over shares, debt, commodities and beyond.
- a. 7-Eleven
- b. 529 plan
- c. 4-4-5 Calendar
- d. Hedge fund

32. _____ is a securities industry term describing the date on which a trade (bonds, equities, foreign exchange, commodities etc) settles. That is, the actual day on which transfer of cash or assets is completed.

It is not necessarily the same as value date (when the settlement amount is calculated.)

- a. Single-index model
- b. Political risk
- c. Mid price
- d. Settlement date

Chapter 2. BUYING AND SELLING SECURITIES

33. The _____ is an American stock exchange. It is the largest electronic screen-based equity securities trading market in the United States. With approximately 3,200 companies, it has more trading volume per day than any other stock exchange in the world.

   a. Nasdaq
   b. 4-4-5 Calendar
   c. 7-Eleven
   d. 529 plan

34. The _____ is usually the number of shares outstanding of a publicly traded company that is sold short, divided by the average daily trading volume (daily transaction).

It is one measure of the market's outlook on a given stock; a higher short interest ratio indicates more pessimism, because a higher proportion of a company's total float has already been sold short.

The short interest and _____ can be deceiving, however, when a company has many convertible securities outstanding and is perceived to be at risk, because convertible and options arbitrageurs will often sell the stock short to manage risk with their long positions in these other instruments.

   a. Short selling
   b. 4-4-5 Calendar
   c. 529 plan
   d. Short ratio

35. _____ is a fee paid on borrowed assets. It is the price paid for the use of borrowed money , or, money earned by deposited funds . Assets that are sometimes lent with _____ include money, shares, consumer goods through hire purchase, major assets such as aircraft, and even entire factories in finance lease arrangements.

   a. A Random Walk Down Wall Street
   b. Insolvency
   c. AAB
   d. Interest

Chapter 3. SECURITY MARKETS

1. An _____ is a contract written by a seller that conveys to the buyer the right -- but not the obligation -- to buy (in the case of a call _____) or to sell (in the case of a put _____) a particular asset, such as a piece of property such as, among others, a futures contract. In return for granting the _____, the seller collects a payment (the premium) from the buyer.

For example, buying a call _____ provides the right to buy a specified quantity of a security at a set strike price at some time on or before expiration, while buying a put _____ provides the right to sell.

   a. Amortization
   b. AT'T Mobility LLC
   c. Annuity
   d. Option

2. A _____ is a fungible, negotiable instrument representing financial value. They are broadly categorized into debt securities (such as banknotes, bonds and debentures), and equity securities; e.g., common stocks. The company or other entity issuing the _____ is called the issuer.
   a. Book entry
   b. Tracking stock
   c. Security
   d. Securities lending

3. A _____, securities exchange or (in Europe) bourse is a corporation or mutual organization which provides 'trading' facilities for stock brokers and traders, to trade stocks and other securities. _____s also provide facilities for the issue and redemption of securities as well as other financial instruments and capital events including the payment of income and dividends. The securities traded on a _____ include: shares issued by companies, unit trusts and other pooled investment products and bonds.
   a. Stock Exchange
   b. 529 plan
   c. 4-4-5 Calendar
   d. 7-Eleven

4. _____ is a measure of the ability of a debtor to pay their debts as and when they fall due. It is usually expressed as a ratio or a percentage of current liabilities.

For a corporation with a published balance sheet there are various ratios used to calculate a measure of liquidity.

   a. Accounting liquidity
   b. Operating leverage
   c. Invested capital
   d. Operating profit margin

5. The _____ is a stock exchange based in New York City, New York. It is the largest stock exchange in the world by dollar value of its listed companies securities. As of October 2008, the combined capitalization of all domestic _____ listed companies was $10.1 trillion.
   a. New York Stock Exchange
   b. 7-Eleven
   c. 529 plan
   d. 4-4-5 Calendar

6. A _____ is an order to buy a security at no more (or sell at no less) than a specific price. This gives the customer some control over the price at which the trade is executed, but may prevent the order from being executed ('filled'.)

A buy _____ can only be executed by the broker at the limit price or lower.

   a. Commercial mortgage-backed securities
   b. Block premium
   c. Limit order
   d. Common stock

Chapter 3. SECURITY MARKETS

7. A _____ is a member of an exchange who is an employee of a member firm and executes orders, as agent, on the floor of the exchange for clients. The _____ receives an order via teletype machine from his firm's trading department and then proceeds to the appropriate trading post on the exchange floor. There he joins other brokers and the specialist in the security being bought or sold and executes the trade at the best competitive price available.
   a. Multivariate normal distribution
   b. Floor broker
   c. Business valuation standards
   d. Case-Shiller Home Price Indices

8. A _____ is a firm that quotes both a buy and a sell price in a financial instrument or commodity, hoping to make a profit on the bid/offer spread, or turn.

   In foreign exchange trading, where most deals are conducted over-the-counter and are, therefore, completely virtual, the _____ sells to and buys from its clients. Hence, the client's loss and the spread is the _____ firm's profit, which gets thus compensated for the effort of providing liquidity in a competitive market.

   a. 4-4-5 Calendar
   b. 7-Eleven
   c. 529 plan
   d. Market maker

9. A _____ is a process of buying and selling goods when potential buyers submit their bids and potential sellers simultaneously submit their ask prices to an auctioneer, and then an auctioneer chooses some price p that clears the market: all the sellers who asked less than p sell and all buyers who bid more than p buy at this price p.
   a. 7-Eleven
   b. 529 plan
   c. 4-4-5 Calendar
   d. Double auction

10. A _____ is a buy or sell order to be executed by the broker immediately at current market prices. As long as there are willing sellers and buyers, _____s are filled.

    A _____ is the simplest of the order types.

    a. Trading curb
    b. Block premium
    c. Stockholder
    d. Market order

11. The _____ is an American stock exchange. It is the largest electronic screen-based equity securities trading market in the United States. With approximately 3,200 companies, it has more trading volume per day than any other stock exchange in the world.
    a. Nasdaq
    b. 529 plan
    c. 4-4-5 Calendar
    d. 7-Eleven

12. _____ is the difference between price and the costs of bringing to market whatever it is that is accounted as an enterprise (whether by harvest, extraction, manufacture, or purchase) in terms of the component costs of delivered goods and/or services and any operating or other expenses.

    A key difficulty in measuring profit is in defining costs. Pure economic monetary profits can be zero or negative even in competitive equilibrium when accounted monetized costs exceed monetized price.

Chapter 3. SECURITY MARKETS

a. Economic profit
b. A Random Walk Down Wall Street
c. AAB
d. Accounting profit

13. _____ is casually defined as the use of computers in stock markets to engage in arbitrage and portfolio insurance strategies. However, the New York Stock Exchange (NYSE) defines the term as 'a wide range of portfolio trading strategies involving the purchase or sale of 15 or more stocks having a total market value of $1 million or more' without any direct reference to the use of computers. The word 'program' can be interpreted in its earlier, more general meaning of a defined and pre-arranged sequence of steps, rather than specifically a computer program.

a. Stop order
b. Program trading
c. Share price
d. Wash sale

14. The U.S. _____ is an independent agency of the United States government which holds primary responsibility for enforcing the federal securities laws and regulating the securities industry, the nation's stock and options exchanges, and other electronic securities markets. The SEC was created by section 4 of the SEC of 1934 (now codified as 15 U.S.C. Â§ 78d and commonly referred to as the 1934 Act.)

a. 4-4-5 Calendar
b. 7-Eleven
c. 529 plan
d. Securities and Exchange Commission

15. The phrase _____ refers to the aspect of corporate strategy, corporate finance and management dealing with the buying, selling and combining of different companies that can aid, finance, or help a growing company in a given industry grow rapidly without having to create another business entity.

An acquisition, also known as a takeover, is the buying of one company (the 'target') by another. An acquisition may be friendly or hostile.

a. 4-4-5 Calendar
b. 7-Eleven
c. 529 plan
d. Mergers and acquisitions

16. In finance, a _____ is a standardized contract, to buy or sell a specified commodity of standardized quality at a certain date in the future, at a market determined price (the futures price.)

The price is determined by the instantaneous equilibrium between the forces of supply and demand among competing buy and sell orders on the exchange at the time of the purchase or sale of the contract.

In many cases, the items may be such non-traditional 'commodities' as foreign currencies, commercial or government paper [e.g., bonds], or 'baskets' of corporate equity ['stock indices'] or other financial instruments.

a. Repurchase agreement
b. Heston model
c. Financial future
d. Futures contract

17. A _____ is a central financial exchange where people can trade standardized futures contracts; that is, a contract to buy specific quantities of a commodity or financial instrument at a specified price with delivery set at a specified time in the future.

Though the origins of futures trading can supposedly be traced to Ancient Greek or Phoenician times, the first modern organized _____ began in 1710 at the Dojima Rice Exchange in Osaka, Japan.

Chapter 3. SECURITY MARKETS

The United States followed in the early 1800s.

a. 7-Eleven
b. 4-4-5 Calendar
c. 529 plan
d. Futures exchange

18. In the United States, the Financial Industry Regulatory Authority (FINRA) is a self-regulatory organization (SRO) under the Securities Exchange Act of 1934, successor to the _____, Inc.

FINRA is responsible for regulatory oversight of all securities firms that do business with the public; professional training, testing and licensing of registered persons; arbitration and mediation; market regulation by contract for The NASDAQ Stock Market, Inc., the American Stock Exchange LLC, and the International Securities Exchange, LLC; and industry utilities, such as Trade Reporting Facilities and other over-the-counter operations.

a. 7-Eleven
b. National Association of Securities Dealers
c. 4-4-5 Calendar
d. 529 plan

19. _____ is a SEC regulation requiring brokers to guarantee customers the best available ask price when buying securities, and the best available bid price when selling securities. This resulted in the making of the Options linkage plan.

a. 7-Eleven
b. 4-4-5 Calendar
c. 529 plan
d. National Best Bid and Offer

20. _____ trading refers to direct institution-to-institution trading without using the service of broker-dealers. It is impossible to estimate the volume of _____ activity because trades are not subject to reporting requirements. Studies have suggested that several millions shares are traded per day.

a. 529 plan
b. Fourth market
c. 4-4-5 Calendar
d. 7-Eleven

21. The _____ is an electronic quotation system in the United States that displays real-time quotes, last-sale prices, and volume information for many over-the-counter (OTC) equity securities that are not listed on the NASDAQ stock exchange or a national securities exchange. Broker-dealers who subscribe to the system can use the _____ to look up prices or enter quotes for OTC securities.

a. AT'T Inc.
b. Insolvency
c. Internal control
d. OTC Bulletin Board

22. In finance, _____ trading is the trading of exchange listed securities in the over-the-counter (OTC) market. Bernard Madoff was engaged in _____ trading.

a. 7-Eleven
b. 529 plan
c. 4-4-5 Calendar
d. Third market

23. In business and finance, a _____ (also referred to as equity _____) of stock means a _____ of ownership in a corporation (company.) In the plural, stocks is often used as a synonym for _____s especially in the United States, but it is less commonly used that way outside of North America.

In the United Kingdom, South Africa, and Australia, stock can also refer to completely different financial instruments such as government bonds or, less commonly, to all kinds of marketable securities.

Chapter 3. SECURITY MARKETS

a. Margin
c. Bucket shop
b. Procter ' Gamble
d. Share

24. _____ is a standard to measure global business processes that are maintained in multiple business applications and serviced by various outsourcing companies.

Internationally, _____ is assessed, managed and monitored by ICIM, a Chicago-based decision science company.

As all standards, this is also an assessment. However, the difference is that it measures companies on three aspects:

1. Process activity and flow standards
2. Process performance standards
3. Process management standards.

a. 7-Eleven
c. POSIT
b. 529 plan
d. 4-4-5 Calendar

25. In financial markets _____ is the practice in which a broker sells the right to trade with his clients to a dealer, a securities exchange, or other market-maker. These market makers are willing to pay for the right to transact with uninformed traders (often retail investors) in order to trade more profitably. By purchasing uninformed order flow, a dealer can buy at the bid and sell at the ask with little risk of trading at a loss with an informed trader who knows that the market is mispricing the security.

a. 7-Eleven
c. 529 plan
b. 4-4-5 Calendar
d. Payment for order flow

26. The _____ is a capital budgeting metric used by firms to decide whether they should make investments. It is an indicator of the efficiency or quality of an investment, as opposed to net present value (NPV), which indicates value or magnitude.

The IRR is the annualized effective compounded return rate which can be earned on the invested capital, i.e., the yield on the investment.

a. A Random Walk Down Wall Street
c. AAB
b. ABN Amro
d. Internal rate of return

27. In finance, _____, also known as return on investment is the ratio of money gained or lost on an investment relative to the amount of money invested. The amount of money gained or lost may be referred to as interest, profit/loss, gain/loss, or net income/loss. The money invested may be referred to as the asset, capital, principal, or the cost basis of the investment.

a. Doctrine of the Proper Law
c. Composiition of Creditors
b. Stock or scrip dividends
d. Rate of return

28. The _____ is overseen by the _____ Association.

Tape C contains over-the-counter stocks listed on the NASDAQ National Market or NASDAQ Small Cap Market, and is overseen by the OTC/UTP Operating Committee.

   a. Liquidating dividend
   c. Peer group analysis
   b. Consolidated tape
   d. January effect

29. A _____ is the price of a single share of a no. of saleable stocks of the company. Once the stock is purchased, the owner becomes a shareholder of the company that issued the share.
   a. Stock split
   c. Share price
   b. Trading curb
   d. Whisper numbers

30. In banking and finance, _____ denotes all activities from the time a commitment is made for a transaction until it is settled. _____ is necessary because the speed of trades is much faster than the cycle time for completing the underlying transaction.

In its widest sense _____ involves the management of post-trading, pre-settlement credit exposures, to ensure that trades are settled in accordance with market rules, even if a buyer or seller should become insolvent prior to settlement.

   a. Clearing house
   c. Procter ' Gamble
   b. Share
   d. Clearing

31. A _____ is a financial services company that provides clearing and settlement services for financial transactions, usually on a futures exchange, and often acts as central counterparty (the payor actually pays the _____, which then pays the payee). A _____ may also offer novation, the substitution of a new contract or debt for an old, or other credit enhancement services to its members.

The term is also used for banks like Suffolk Bank that acted as a restraint on the over-issuance of private bank notes.

   a. Bucket shop
   c. Valuation
   b. Warrant
   d. Clearing house

32. Established in 1973, The _____ was created to alleviate the rising volumes of paperwork and the lack of security that developed after rapid growth in the volume of transactions in the U.S. securities industry in the late 1960s.

Before _____ and NSCC were formed, brokers physically exchanged certificates, employing hundreds of messengers to carry certificates and checks. The mechanisms brokers used to transfer securities and keep records relied heavily on pen and paper.

   a. Wells Fargo ' Co.
   c. Protect
   b. Federal Home Loan Mortgage Corporation
   d. Depository Trust Company

Chapter 3. SECURITY MARKETS

33. A _____ is a corporation, especially a commercial bank, organized to perform the fiduciary functions of trusts and agencies. It is normally owned by one of three types of structures: an independent partnership, a bank, or a law firm, each of which specializes in being a trustee of various kinds of trusts and in managing estates.
   a. Person-to-person lending
   b. Savings and loan association
   c. Mutual fund
   d. Trust Company

34. The institution most often referenced by the word '_____' is a public or publicly traded _____, the shares of which are traded on a public stock exchange (e.g., the New York Stock Exchange or Nasdaq in the United States) where shares of stock of _____s are bought and sold by and to the general public. Most of the largest businesses in the world are publicly traded _____s. However, the majority of _____s are said to be closely held, privately held or close _____s, meaning that no ready market exists for the trading of shares.
   a. Depository Trust Company
   b. Corporation
   c. Federal Home Loan Mortgage Corporation
   d. Protect

35. The _____ of 1970 codified at 15 U.S.C. § 78aaa through 15 U.S.C. § 78lll, established the Securities Investor Protection Corporation (SIPC). Most brokers and dealers registered under the Securities Exchange Act of 1934 are required to be members of the SIPC.

The SIPC maintains a fund that is intended to protect investors against the misappropriation of their funds and of most types of securities in the event of the failure of their broker.

   a. McFadden Act
   b. Securities Investor Protection Act
   c. Fiduciary
   d. Quiet period

36. The _____ is a federally mandated non-profit corporation in the United States that protects securities investors from harm if a broker-dealer company fails. Investors are not insured for any potential loss while invested in the market.

Congress created _____ in 1970 through the Securities Investor Protection Act (15 U.S.C.

   a. Securities Investor Protection Corporation
   b. Prudent man rule
   c. SIPC
   d. Rule 144A

37. In Modern Portfolio Theory, the _____ is the graphical representation of the Capital Asset Pricing Model. It displays the expected rate of return for an overall market as a function of systematic (non-diversifiable) risk (beta.)

The Y-Intercept (beta=0) of the _____ is equal to the risk-free interest rate.

   a. Certificate in Investment Performance Measurement
   b. Rebalancing
   c. Divestment
   d. Security market line

38. A _____ or market-based mechanism is any of a wide variety of ways to match up buyers and sellers.

An example of a _____ uses announced bid and ask prices. Generally speaking, when two parties wish to engage in a trade, the purchaser will announce a price he is willing to pay (the bid price) and seller will announce a price he is willing to accept (the ask price).

Chapter 3. SECURITY MARKETS

a. 4-4-5 Calendar
c. 7-Eleven
b. 529 plan
d. Price mechanism

39. The _____ for securities is the difference between the price quoted by a market maker for an immediate sale and an immediate purchase The size of the bid-offer spread in a given commodity is a measure of the liquidity of the market.

The trader initiating the transaction is said to demand liquidity, and the other party to the transaction supplies liquidity.

a. Capital outflow
c. Trade-off
b. Defined contribution plan
d. Bid/offer spread

40. In economics and related disciplines, a _____ is a cost incurred in making an economic exchange. For example, most people, when buying or selling a stock, must pay a commission to their broker; that commission is a _____ of doing the stock deal. Or consider buying a banana from a store; to purchase the banana, your costs will be not only the price of the banana itself, but also the energy and effort it requires to find out which of the various banana products you prefer, where to get them and at what price, the cost of traveling from your house to the store and back, the time waiting in line, and the effort of the paying itself; the costs above and beyond the cost of the banana are the _____s.

a. Marginal cost
c. Transaction cost
b. Variable costs
d. Fixed costs

41. In economics, business, and accounting, a _____ is the value of money that has been used up to produce something, and hence is not available for use anymore. In business, the _____ may be one of acquisition, in which case the amount of money expended to acquire it is counted as _____. In this case, money is the input that is gone in order to acquire the thing.

a. Marginal cost
c. Sliding scale fees
b. Fixed costs
d. Cost

42. _____ is a measurement of corporate or economic size equal to the share price times the number of shares outstanding of a public company. As owning stock represents owning the company, including all its equity, capitalization could represent the public opinion of a company's net worth and is a determining factor in stock valuation. Likewise, the capitalization of stock markets or economic regions may be compared to other economic indicators.

a. Just-in-time
c. Synthetic CDO
b. Proxy fight
d. Market capitalization

43. An _____ is a company whose main business is holding securities of other companies purely for investment purposes. The _____ invests money on behalf of its shareholders who in turn share in the profits and losses.

a. AAB
c. Unit investment trust
b. A Random Walk Down Wall Street
d. Investment Company

44. A _____ is a professionally managed type of collective investment scheme that pools money from many investors and invests it in stocks, bonds, short-term money market instruments, and/or other securities. The _____ will have a fund manager that trades the pooled money on a regular basis. Currently, the worldwide value of all _____s totals more than $26 trillion.

Chapter 3. SECURITY MARKETS

Since 1940, there have been three basic types of investment companies in the United States: open-end funds, also known in the US as _____s; unit investment trusts (UITs); and closed-end funds.

- a. Financial intermediary
- b. Net asset value
- c. Trust company
- d. Mutual fund

45. The _____ of 1934 is a law governing the secondary trading of securities (stocks, bonds, and debentures) in the United States of America. The Act, 48 Stat. 881 (enacted June 6, 1934), codified at 15 U.S.C. Â§ 78a et seq., was a sweeping piece of legislation. The Act and related statutes form the basis of regulation of the financial markets and their participants in the United States.
- a. 4-4-5 Calendar
- b. 529 plan
- c. 7-Eleven
- d. Securities Exchange Act

46. A _____ is a state law in the United States that regulates the offering and sale of securities to protect the public from fraud. Though the specific provisions of these laws vary among states, they all require the registration of all securities offerings and sales, as well as of stock brokers and brokerage firms. Each state's _____ is administered by its appropriate regulatory agency, and most also provide private causes of action for private investors who have been injured by securities fraud.
- a. Blue sky law
- b. Patent
- c. Bundesrechnungshof
- d. Court of Audit of Belgium

47. The _____ of 1933 established the Federal Deposit Insurance Corporation (FDIC) in the United States and included banking reforms, some of which were designed to control speculation. Some provisions such as Regulation Q, which allowed the Federal Reserve to regulate interest rates in savings accounts, were repealed by the Depository Institutions Deregulation and Monetary Control Act of 1980. Provisions that prohibit a bank holding company from owning other financial companies were repealed on November 12, 1999, by the Gramm-Leach-Bliley Act.
- a. 529 plan
- b. Glass-Steagall Act
- c. 7-Eleven
- d. 4-4-5 Calendar

Chapter 4. EFFICIENT MARKETS, INVESTMENT VALUE, AND MARKET PRICE

1. A _____, securities exchange or (in Europe) bourse is a corporation or mutual organization which provides 'trading' facilities for stock brokers and traders, to trade stocks and other securities. _____s also provide facilities for the issue and redemption of securities as well as other financial instruments and capital events including the payment of income and dividends. The securities traded on a _____ include: shares issued by companies, unit trusts and other pooled investment products and bonds.
   a. 7-Eleven
   b. Stock Exchange
   c. 529 plan
   d. 4-4-5 Calendar

2. A _____, is a mathematical formalization of a trajectory that consists of taking successive random steps. The results of _____ analysis have been applied to computer science, physics, ecology, economics and a number of other fields as a fundamental model for random processes in time. For example, the path traced by a molecule as it travels in a liquid or a gas, the search path of a foraging animal, the price of a fluctuating stock and the financial status of a gambler can all be modeled as _____s.
   a. 7-Eleven
   b. 529 plan
   c. 4-4-5 Calendar
   d. Random walk

3. A _____ is a fungible, negotiable instrument representing financial value. They are broadly categorized into debt securities (such as banknotes, bonds and debentures), and equity securities; e.g., common stocks. The company or other entity issuing the _____ is called the issuer.
   a. Security
   b. Book entry
   c. Securities lending
   d. Tracking stock

4. In economics, business, and accounting, a _____ is the value of money that has been used up to produce something, and hence is not available for use anymore. In business, the _____ may be one of acquisition, in which case the amount of money expended to acquire it is counted as _____. In this case, money is the input that is gone in order to acquire the thing.
   a. Marginal cost
   b. Sliding scale fees
   c. Fixed costs
   d. Cost

5. In economics and related disciplines, a _____ is a cost incurred in making an economic exchange. For example, most people, when buying or selling a stock, must pay a commission to their broker; that commission is a _____ of doing the stock deal. Or consider buying a banana from a store; to purchase the banana, your costs will be not only the price of the banana itself, but also the energy and effort it requires to find out which of the various banana products you prefer, where to get them and at what price, the cost of traveling from your house to the store and back, the time waiting in line, and the effort of the paying itself; the costs above and beyond the cost of the banana are the _____s.
   a. Variable costs
   b. Marginal cost
   c. Transaction cost
   d. Fixed costs

6. _____ refers to a portfolio management strategy where the manager makes specific investments with the goal of outperforming an investment benchmark index. Investors or mutual funds that do not aspire to create a return in excess of a benchmark index will often invest in an index fund that replicates as closely as possible the investment weighting and returns of that index; this is called passive management. _____ is the opposite of passive management, because in passive management the manager does not seek to outperform the benchmark index.
   a. A Random Walk Down Wall Street
   b. AAB
   c. ABN Amro
   d. Active management

Chapter 4. EFFICIENT MARKETS, INVESTMENT VALUE, AND MARKET PRICE

7. An _____ is a statistical method to assess the impact of an event on the value of a firm. For example, the announcement of a merger between two firms can be analyzed to see whether investors believe the merger will create or destroy value. Event studies have been used in a large variety of studies, including [mergers and acquisitions], earnings announcements, debt or equity issues, corporate reorganisations, investment decisions and corporate social responsibility (MacKinlay 1997; McWilliams ' Siegel, 1997.)

   a. AAB
   b. Event study
   c. ABN Amro
   d. A Random Walk Down Wall Street

8. _____ is a financial strategy in which a fund manager makes as few portfolio decisions as possible, in order to minimize transaction costs, including the incidence of capital gains tax. One popular method is to mimic the performance of an externally specified index--called 'index funds'. The ethos of an index fund is aptly summed up in the injunction to an index fund manager: 'Don't just do something, sit there!'

   _____ is most common on the equity market, where index funds track a stock market index, but it is becoming more common in other investment types, including bonds, commodities and hedge funds.

   a. Net asset value
   b. Passive Management
   c. Trust company
   d. Savings and loan association

9.

   In finance, the _____ can be the expected rate of return above the risk-free interest rate. When measuring risk, a common sense approach is to compare the risk-free return on T-bills and the very risky return on other investments. The difference between these two returns can be interpreted as a measure of the excess return on the average risky asset. This excess return is known as the _____.

   a. Risk modeling
   b. Risk premium
   c. Risk adjusted return on capital
   d. Risk aversion

Chapter 5. THE VALUATION OF RISKLESS SECURITIES

1. In finance and economics _____ refers to the rate of interest before adjustment for inflation (in contrast with the real interest rate); or, for interest balls stated' without adjustment for the full effect of compounding (also referred to as the nominal annual rate.) An interest rate is called nominal if the frequency of compounding (e.g. a month) is not identical to the basic time unit (normally a year.)

The real interest rate includes compensation for the lender's lost value due to inflation, whereas the _____ excludes inflation.

   a. Nominal interest rate
   b. Shanghai Interbank Offered Rate
   c. SIBOR
   d. Cash accumulation equation

2. _____ is a fee paid on borrowed assets. It is the price paid for the use of borrowed money, or, money earned by deposited funds. Assets that are sometimes lent with _____ include money, shares, consumer goods through hire purchase, major assets such as aircraft, and even entire factories in finance lease arrangements.
   a. A Random Walk Down Wall Street
   b. Interest
   c. Insolvency
   d. AAB

3. An _____ is the price a borrower pays for the use of money they do not own, and the return a lender receives for deferring the use of funds, by lending it to the borrower. _____s are normally expressed as a percentage rate over the period of one year.

   _____s targets are also a vital tool of monetary policy and are used to control variables like investment, inflation, and unemployment.

   a. ABN Amro
   b. A Random Walk Down Wall Street
   c. AAB
   d. Interest rate

4. The '_____' is approximately the nominal interest rate minus the inflation rate Since the inflation rate over the course of a loan is not known initially, volatility in inflation represents a risk to both the lender and the borrower.

   In economics and finance, an individual who lends money for repayment at a later point in time expects to be compensated for the time value of money, or not having the use of that money while it is lent.

   a. 529 plan
   b. Real interest rate
   c. 4-4-5 Calendar
   d. 7-Eleven

5. A _____ is a fungible, negotiable instrument representing financial value. They are broadly categorized into debt securities (such as banknotes, bonds and debentures), and equity securities; e.g., common stocks. The company or other entity issuing the _____ is called the issuer.
   a. Tracking stock
   b. Book entry
   c. Securities lending
   d. Security

6. A _____ is a measure of the average price of consumer goods and services purchased by households. The _____ can be used to index (i.e., adjust for the effects of inflation) wages, salaries, pensions, or regulated or contracted prices. The _____ is, along with the population census and the National Income and Product Accounts, one of the most closely watched national economic statistics.

Chapter 5. THE VALUATION OF RISKLESS SECURITIES

a. Divisia index
b. Consumer Price Index
c. 529 plan
d. 4-4-5 Calendar

7. A _____ is a theoretical price index that measures relative cost of living over time. It is an index that measures differences in the price of goods and services, and allows for substitutions to other items as prices change.

There are many different methodologies that have been developed to approximate _____ es, including methods that allow for substitution among items as relative prices change.

a. Cost-of-living index
b. 7-Eleven
c. 4-4-5 Calendar
d. 529 plan

8. The _____ in financial mathematics and economics estimates the relationship between nominal and real interest rates under inflation. It is named after Irving Fisher who was famous for his works on the theory of interest. In finance, the _____ is primarily used in YTM calculations of bonds or IRR calculations of investments.

Letting r denote the real interest rate, i denote the nominal interest rate, and let $>\pi$ denote the inflation rate, the _____ is:

a. Treynor-Black model
b. Fisher equation
c. Binomial options pricing model
d. Discount rate

9. A _____ is a normalized average (typically a weighted average) of prices for a given class of goods or services in a given region, during a given interval of time. It is a statistic designed to help to compare how these prices, taken as a whole, differ between time periods or geographical locations.

a. Transfer pricing
b. Price Index
c. Price discrimination
d. Discounts and allowances

10. The coupon or _____ of a bond is the amount of interest paid per year expressed as a percentage of the face value of the bond.

For example if you hold $10,000 nominal of a bond described as a 4.5% loan stock, you will receive $450 in interest each year (probably in two installments of $225 each.)

Not all bonds have coupons.

a. Zero-coupon bond
b. Coupon rate
c. Revenue bonds
d. Puttable bond

11. A _____ is a bond bought at a price lower than its face value, with the face value repaid at the time of maturity. It does not make periodic interest payments, or have so-called 'coupons,' hence the term _____. Investors earn return from the compounded interest all paid at maturity plus the difference between the discounted price of the bond and its par value.

32   *Chapter 5. THE VALUATION OF RISKLESS SECURITIES*

a. Zero-coupon bond
b. Clean price
c. Corporate bond
d. Bond fund

12. In finance, a _____ is a debt security, in which the authorized issuer owes the holders a debt and, depending on the terms of the _____, is obliged to pay interest (the coupon) and/or to repay the principal at a later date, termed maturity.

Thus a _____ is a loan: the issuer is the borrower, the _____ holder is the lender, and the coupon is the interest. _____s provide the borrower with external funds to finance long-term investments, or, in the case of government _____s, to finance current expenditure.

a. Catastrophe bonds
b. Convertible bond
c. Puttable bond
d. Bond

13. Accrual, in accounting, describes the accounting method known as _____, whereby revenues and expenses are recognized when they are accrued, i.e. accumulated (earned or incurred), regardless when the actual cash is received or paid out.

E.g. a company delivers a product to a customer who will pay for it 30 days later in the next fiscal year starting a week after the delivery. The company recognizes the proceeds as a revenue in its current income statement still for the fiscal year of the delivery, even though it will get paid in cash during the following accounting period.

a. ABN Amro
b. A Random Walk Down Wall Street
c. AAB
d. Accrual basis

14. _____ is a system of tracking ownership of securities where no certificate is given to investors. In the case of _____ only issues, while investors do not receive certificates, a custodian holds one or more global certificates. Dematerialized securities, in contrast are ones in which no certificates exist (instead, the security issuer or its agent keeps records, usually electronically, of who holds outstanding securities.)

a. Securities lending
b. Marketable
c. Tracking stock
d. Book entry

15. _____ are government bonds issued by the United States Department of the Treasury through the Bureau of the Public Debt. They are the debt financing instruments of the U.S. Federal government, and they are often referred to simply as Treasuries or Treasurys. There are four types of marketable _____: Treasury bills, Treasury notes, Treasury bonds, and Treasury Inflation Protected Securities (TIPS.)

a. 4-4-5 Calendar
b. Treasury Securities
c. Treasury Inflation Protected Securities
d. Treasury Inflation-Protected Securities

16. The _____ or redemption yield is the yield promised to the bondholder on the assumption that the bond or other fixed-interest security such as gilts will be held to maturity, that all coupon and principal payments will be made and coupon payments are reinvested at the bond's promised yield at the same rate as invested. It is a measure of the return of the bond. This technique in theory allows investors to calculate the fair value of different financial instruments.

a. 4-4-5 Calendar
b. Yield to maturity
c. Macaulay duration
d. Yield

Chapter 5. THE VALUATION OF RISKLESS SECURITIES

17. _____ is a method for constructing a (zero-coupon) fixed-income yield curve from the prices of a set of coupon-bearing products by forward substitution.

Using these zero-coupon products it becomes possible to derive par swap rates (forward and spot) for all maturities by making a few assumptions (including linear interpolation.) The term structure of spot returns is recovered from the bond yields by solving for them recursively, this iterative process is called the BootStrap Method.

a. Probability of default
c. Bullet loan
b. Reserve requirement
d. Bootstrapping

18. The _____ of a commodity, a security or a currency is the price that is quoted for immediate (spot) settlement (payment and delivery.) Spot settlement is normally one or two business days from trade date. This is in contrast with the forward price established in a forward contract or futures contract, where contract terms (price) are set now, but delivery and payment will occur at a future date.

a. Long position
c. Limits to arbitrage
b. Market anomaly
d. Spot rate

19. A '_____' is a 'Charge' that is paid to obtain the right to delay a payment. Essentially, the payer purchases the right to make a given payment in the future instead of in the Present. The '_____', or 'Charge' that must be paid to delay the payment, is simply the difference between what the payment amount would be if it were paid in the present and what the payment amount would be paid if it were paid in the future.

a. Discount
c. Risk aversion
b. Value at risk
d. Risk modeling

20. The _____, P(T), is the number which a future cash flow, to be received at time T, must be multiplied by in order to obtain the current present value. Thus, a fixed annually compounded discount rate is

$$P(T) = \frac{1}{(1+r)^T}$$

For fixed continuously compounded discount rate we have

$$P(T) = e^{-rT}$$

For discounts in marketing, see discounts and allowances, sales promotion, and pricing.

a. Discount
c. Risk premium
b. Risk modeling
d. Discount factor

21. The _____ or forward rate is the agreed upon price of an asset in a forward contract. Using the rational pricing assumption, we can express the _____ in terms of the spot price and any dividends etc., so that there is no possibility for arbitrage.

Chapter 5. THE VALUATION OF RISKLESS SECURITIES

The _____ is given by:

$$F = e^{(r+q)T} \left(S_0 - \sum_i D_i e^{-(r+q)t_i} \right)$$

where

F is the _____ to be paid at time T
e^x is the exponential function
r is the risk-free interest rate
q is the cost-of-carry
S_0 is the spot price of the asset (i.e. what it would sell for at time 0)
D_i is a dividend which is guaranteed to be paid at time t_i where $0 < t_i < T$.

The two questions here are what price the short position (the seller of the asset) should offer to maximize his gain, and what price the long position (the buyer of the asset) should accept to maximize his gain?

At the very least we know that both do not want to lose any money in the deal.

a. Security interest
b. Forward price
c. Biweekly Mortgage
d. Financial Gerontology

22. A _____ is an agreement between two parties to buy or sell an asset at a specified point of time in the future. The price of the underlying instrument, in whatever form, is paid before control of the instrument changes. This is one of the many forms of buy/sell orders where the time of trade is not the time where the securities themselves are exchanged.
a. Loan Credit Default Swap Index
b. Constant maturity credit default swap
c. Forward contract
d. Derivatives markets

23. A _____ is an exchange of promises between two or more parties to do an act which is enforceable in a court of law. It is where an unqualified offer meets a qualified acceptance and the parties reach Consensus ad Idem. The parties must have the necessary capacity to _____ and the _____ must not be either trifling, indeterminate, impossible or illegal.
a. Contract
b. 529 plan
c. 4-4-5 Calendar
d. 7-Eleven

24. _____ is the concept of adding accumulated interest back to the principal, so that interest is earned on interest from that moment on. The act of declaring interest to be principal is called compounding (i.e., interest is compounded.) A loan, for example, may have its interest compounded every month: in this case, a loan with $100 principal and 1% interest per month would have a balance of $101 at the end of the first month.
a. Penny stock
b. 4-4-5 Calendar
c. Risk management
d. Compound interest

25. The _____ for an investment is a calculated annual yield for an investment, which may not pay out yearly. This allows investments which payout with different frequencies to be compared.

Chapter 5. THE VALUATION OF RISKLESS SECURITIES

a. 4-4-5 Calendar
c. Bond equivalent yield
b. 529 plan
d. 7-Eleven

26. In finance, the term _____ describes the amount in cash that returns to the owners of a security. Normally it does not include the price variations, at the difference of the total return. _____ applies to various stated rates of return on stocks (common and preferred, and convertible), fixed income instruments (bonds, notes, bills, strips, zero coupon), and some other investment type insurance products (e.g. annuities.)
   a. Yield to maturity
   c. Macaulay duration
   b. 4-4-5 Calendar
   d. Yield

27. In finance, the _____ is the relation between the interest rate (or cost of borrowing) and the time to maturity of the debt for a given borrower in a given currency. For example, the current U.S. dollar interest rates paid on U.S. Treasury securities for various maturities are closely watched by many traders, and are commonly plotted on a graph such as the one on the right which is informally called 'the _____.' More formal mathematical descriptions of this relation are often called the term structure of interest rates.

The yield of a debt instrument is the annualized percentage increase in the value of the investment.

   a. 4-4-5 Calendar
   c. 7-Eleven
   b. Yield curve
   d. 529 plan

28. In economics, _____ is a rise in the general level of prices of goods and services in an economy over a period of time. The term '_____' once referred to increases in the money supply (monetary _____); however, economic debates about the relationship between money supply and price levels have led to its primary use today in describing price _____. _____ can also be described as a decline in the real value of money--a loss of purchasing power in the medium of exchange which is also the monetary unit of account.
   a. Inflation
   c. ABN Amro
   b. A Random Walk Down Wall Street
   d. AAB

29. _____ is a measure of the ability of a debtor to pay their debts as and when they fall due. It is usually expressed as a ratio or a percentage of current liabilities.

For a corporation with a published balance sheet there are various ratios used to calculate a measure of liquidity.

   a. Invested capital
   c. Operating leverage
   b. Operating profit margin
   d. Accounting liquidity

30. John Maynard Keynes developed the _____ of Interest in the General Theory of Employment Interest and Money. The primary consideration of the _____ is the demand for money as an asset, as a means for holding wealth. Interest rates, he argues, cannot be a reward for savings as such because, if a person hoards his savings in cash, keeping it under his mattress say, he will receive no interest, although he has nevertheless, refrained from consuming all his current income.
   a. 529 plan
   c. 7-Eleven
   b. 4-4-5 Calendar
   d. Liquidity preference

31. _____ is a term used to explain a difference between two types of financial securities (e.g. stocks), that have all the same qualities except liquidity. For example:

Chapter 5. THE VALUATION OF RISKLESS SECURITIES

_____ is a segment of a three-part theory that works to explain the behavior of yield curves for interest rates. The upwards-curving component of the interest yield can be explained by the _____.

a. Liquidity premium
c. 4-4-5 Calendar

b. 7-Eleven
d. 529 plan

32. The _____, interest yield, income yield, flat yield or running yield is a financial term used in reference to bonds and other fixed-interest securities such as gilts. It is the ratio of the annual interest payment and the bond's current price.

The _____ only therefore refers to the yield of the bond at the current moment. It does not reflect the total return over the life of the bond. In particular, it takes no account of reinvestment risk (the uncertainty about the rate at which future cashflows can be reinvested) or the fact that bonds usually mature at par value, which can be an important component of a bond's return.

a. Perpetuity
c. Modified Internal Rate of Return

b. Stochastic volatility
d. Current yield

Chapter 6. THE PORTFOLIO SELECTION PROBLEM

1. The _____ is the weighted-average most likely outcome in gambling, probability theory, economics or finance.

   In gambling and probability theory, there is usually a discrete set of possible outcomes. In this case, _____ is a measure of the relative balance of win or loss weighted by their chances of occurring.

   a. A Random Walk Down Wall Street
   b. Expected return
   c. ABN Amro
   d. AAB

2. _____ proposes how rational investors will use diversification to optimize their portfolios, and how a risky asset should be priced. The basic concepts of the theory are Markowitz diversification, the efficient frontier, capital asset pricing model, the alpha and beta coefficients, the Capital Market Line and the Securities Market Line.

   _____ models an asset's return as a random variable, and models a portfolio as a weighted combination of assets so that the return of a portfolio is the weighted combination of the assets' returns.

   a. Payback period
   b. Consumer basket
   c. Market value
   d. Modern portfolio theory

3. In statistics, _____ has two related meanings:

   - the arithmetic _____
   - the expected value of a random variable, which is also called the population _____.

   It is sometimes stated that the '_____' is average. This is incorrect if '_____' is taken in the specific sense of 'arithmetic _____' as there are different types of averages: the _____, median, and mode. Other simple statistical analyses use measures of spread, such as range, interquartile range, or standard deviation. For a real-valued random variable X, the _____ is the expectation of X. Note that not every probability distribution has a defined _____; see the Cauchy distribution for an example.

   a. Probability distribution
   b. Harmonic mean
   c. Mean
   d. Sample size

4. In mathematics, _____ are used in the study of chance and probability. They were developed to assist in the analysis of games of chance, stochastic events, and the results of scientific experiments by capturing only the mathematical properties necessary to answer probabilistic questions. Further formalizations have firmly grounded the entity in the theoretical domains of mathematics by making use of measure theory.
   a. Variance
   b. Standard deviation
   c. Monte Carlo methods
   d. Random variables

5. In finance, _____, also known as return on investment is the ratio of money gained or lost on an investment relative to the amount of money invested. The amount of money gained or lost may be referred to as interest, profit/loss, gain/loss, or net income/loss. The money invested may be referred to as the asset, capital, principal, or the cost basis of the investment.
   a. Doctrine of the Proper Law
   b. Stock or scrip dividends
   c. Composiition of Creditors
   d. Rate of return

Chapter 6. THE PORTFOLIO SELECTION PROBLEM

6. In probability and statistics, the _____ of a collection of numbers is a measure of the dispersion of the numbers from their expected (mean) value. It can apply to a probability distribution, a random variable, a population or a data set. The _____ is usually denoted with the letter σ (lowercase sigma.)
   a. Sample size
   b. Standard deviation
   c. Kurtosis
   d. Mean

7. In economics, the _____ of a good or of a service is the utility of the specific use to which an agent would put a given increase in that good or service, or of the specific use that would be abandoned in response to a given decrease. In other words, _____ is the utility of the marginal use -- which, on the assumption of economic rationality, would be the least urgent use of the good or service, from the best feasible combination of actions in which its use is included. Under the mainstream assumptions, the _____ of a good or service is the posited quantified change in utility obtained by increasing or by decreasing use of that good or service.
   a. 529 plan
   b. 7-Eleven
   c. Marginal utility
   d. 4-4-5 Calendar

8. _____ is a concept in economics, finance, and psychology related to the behaviour of consumers and investors under uncertainty. _____ is the reluctance of a person to accept a bargain with an uncertain payoff rather than another bargain with a more certain, but possibly lower, expected payoff.

   The inverse of a person's _____ is sometimes called their risk tolerance

   a. Risk premium
   b. Discount factor
   c. Risk adjusted return on capital
   d. Risk aversion

9. In economics, _____ is a measure of the relative satisfaction from or desirability of consumption of various goods and services. Given this measure, one may speak meaningfully of increasing or decreasing _____, and thereby explain economic behavior in terms of attempts to increase one's _____. For illustrative purposes, changes in _____ are sometimes expressed in units called utils.
   a. AAB
   b. A Random Walk Down Wall Street
   c. Utility function
   d. Utility

10. The _____ is the guaranteed payoff at which a person is 'indifferent' between accepting the guaranteed payoff and a higher but uncertain payoff. (It is the amount of the higher payout minus the risk premium).
    a. Certainty equivalent
    b. 529 plan
    c. 7-Eleven
    d. 4-4-5 Calendar

11. In microeconomic theory, an _____ is a graph showing different bundles of goods, each measured as to quantity, between which a consumer is indifferent. That is, at each point on the curve, the consumer has no preference for one bundle over another. In other words, they are all equally preferred. One can equivalently refer to each point on the _____ as rendering the same level of utility (satisfaction) for the consumer.
    a. A Random Walk Down Wall Street
    b. AAB
    c. Indifference curve
    d. ABN Amro

12.

Chapter 6. THE PORTFOLIO SELECTION PROBLEM

In finance, the _____ can be the expected rate of return above the risk-free interest rate. When measuring risk, a common sense approach is to compare the risk-free return on T-bills and the very risky return on other investments. The difference between these two returns can be interpreted as a measure of the excess return on the average risky asset. This excess return is known as the _____.

a. Risk premium
b. Risk adjusted return on capital
c. Risk aversion
d. Risk modeling

13. Behavioral economics and _____ are closely related fields that have evolved to be a separate branch of economic and financial analysis which applies scientific research on human and social, cognitive and emotional factors to better understand economic decisions by, say, consumers, borrowers, investors, and how they affect market prices, returns and the allocation of resources.

The field is primarily concerned with the bounds of rationality (selfishness, self-control) of economic agents. Behavioral models typically integrate insights from psychology with neo-classical economic theory.

a. Market structure
b. Recession
c. Behavioral finance
d. Medium of exchange

14. A _____ is a fungible, negotiable instrument representing financial value. They are broadly categorized into debt securities (such as banknotes, bonds and debentures), and equity securities; e.g., common stocks. The company or other entity issuing the _____ is called the issuer.

a. Security
b. Book entry
c. Tracking stock
d. Securities lending

15. In probability theory and statistics, a _____ identifies either the probability of each value of an unidentified random variable (when the variable is discrete), or the probability of the value falling within a particular interval (when the variable is continuous.) The _____ describes the range of possible values that a random variable can attain and the probability that the value of the random variable is within any (measurable) subset of that range. The Normal distribution, often called the 'bell curve'

When the random variable takes values in the set of real numbers, the _____ is completely described by the cumulative distribution function, whose value at each real x is the probability that the random variable is smaller than or equal to x.

a. Correlation
b. P-value
c. Standard deviation
d. Probability distribution

16. The _____ is an important family of continuous probability distributions, applicable in many fields. Each member of the family may be defined by two parameters, location and scale: the mean and variance respectively. The standard _____ is the _____ with a mean of zero and a variance of one

a. Correlation
b. Probability distribution
c. Random variables
d. Normal distribution

17. In probability theory and statistics, _____ indicates the strength and direction of a linear relationship between two random variables. That is in contrast with the usage of the term in colloquial speech, which denotes any relationship, not necessarily linear. In general statistical usage, _____ or co-relation refers to the departure of two random variables from independence.

    a. Variance
    b. Probability distribution
    c. Geometric mean
    d. Correlation

18. In probability theory and statistics, _____ is a measure of how much two variables change together (variance is a special case of the _____ when the two variables are identical.)

If two variables tend to vary together (that is, when one of them is above its expected value, then the other variable tends to be above its expected value too), then the _____ between the two variables will be positive. On the other hand, when one of them is above its expected value the other variable tends to be below its expected value, then the _____ between the two variables will be negative.

    a. Probability distribution
    b. Covariance
    c. Frequency distribution
    d. Stratified sampling

19. In spatial statistics, the empirical _____ is described by

where z is a datum at a particular location, h is the distance between ordered data, and n(h) is the number of paired data at a distance of h. The _____ is half the variance of the increments $z(x_i + h) >- z(x_i)$, but the whole variance of z-values at given separation distance h (Bachmaier and Backes, 2008.)

A plot of _____s versus distances between ordered data in a graph is known as a semivariogram rather than a variogram.

    a. P-value
    b. Mean
    c. Statistics
    d. Semivariance

Chapter 7. PORTFOLIO ANALYSIS

1. The institution most often referenced by the word '_____' is a public or publicly traded _____, the shares of which are traded on a public stock exchange (e.g., the New York Stock Exchange or Nasdaq in the United States) where shares of stock of _____s are bought and sold by and to the general public. Most of the largest businesses in the world are publicly traded _____s. However, the majority of _____s are said to be closely held, privately held or close _____s, meaning that no ready market exists for the trading of shares.
   a. Federal Home Loan Mortgage Corporation
   b. Depository Trust Company
   c. Corporation
   d. Protect

2. Explicit _____ is a measure implemented in many countries to protect bank depositors, in full or in part, from losses caused by a bank's inability to pay its debts when due. _____ systems are one component of a financial system safety net that promotes financial stability.
   a. Time deposit
   b. Deposit Insurance
   c. Banking panic
   d. Reserve requirement

3. The _____ is a United States government corporation created by the Glass-Steagall Act of 1933. It provides deposit insurance, which guarantees the safety of checking and savings deposits in member banks, currently up to $250,000 per depositor per bank. Insured deposits are backed by the full faith and credit of the United States.
   a. Ford Foundation
   b. Federal Deposit Insurance Corporation
   c. FASB
   d. NYSE Group

4. In economics and finance, _____ is the practice of taking advantage of a price differential between two or more markets: striking a combination of matching deals that capitalize upon the imbalance, the profit being the difference between the market prices. When used by academics, an _____ is a transaction that involves no negative cash flow at any probabilistic or temporal state and a positive cash flow in at least one state; in simple terms, a risk-free profit.
   a. Arbitrage
   b. Issuer
   c. Efficient-market hypothesis
   d. Initial margin

5. _____ in finance is a risk management technique, related to hedging, that mixes a wide variety of investments within a portfolio. Because the fluctuations of a single security have less impact on a diverse portfolio, _____ minimizes the risk from any one investment.

   A simple example of _____ is the following: On a particular island the entire economy consists of two companies: one that sells umbrellas and another that sells sunscreen.

   a. 7-Eleven
   b. 4-4-5 Calendar
   c. 529 plan
   d. Diversification

6. _____ is the risk that the value of an investment will decrease due to moves in market factors. The five standard _____ factors are:

   - Equity risk, the risk that stock prices will change.
   - Interest rate risk, the risk that interest rates will change.
   - Currency risk, the risk that foreign exchange rates will change.
   - Commodity risk, the risk that commodity prices (e.g. grains, metals) will change.

Chapter 7. PORTFOLIO ANALYSIS

As with other forms of risk, _____ may be measured in a number of ways. Traditionally, this is done using a Value at Risk methodology. Value at risk is well established as a risk management technique, but it contains a number of limiting assumptions that constrain its accuracy.

a. Tracking error
c. Currency risk
b. Transaction risk
d. Market risk

7. In business and finance, a _____ (also referred to as equity _____) of stock means a _____ of ownership in a corporation (company.) In the plural, stocks is often used as a synonym for _____s especially in the United States, but it is less commonly used that way outside of North America.

In the United Kingdom, South Africa, and Australia, stock can also refer to completely different financial instruments such as government bonds or, less commonly, to all kinds of marketable securities.

a. Share
c. Margin
b. Procter ' Gamble
d. Bucket shop

8. In finance, _____ refers to that segment of risk in an investment portfolio that is due to active management decisions made by the portfolio manager. It does not include any risk (return) that is merely a function of the market's movement. In addition to risk (return) from specific stock selection or industry and factor 'bets', it can also include risk (return) from market-timing decisions.

a. A Random Walk Down Wall Street
c. AAB
b. ABN Amro
d. Active risk

9. An _____ or index tracker is a collective investment scheme (usually a mutual fund or exchange-traded fund) that aims to replicate the movements of an index of a specific financial market regardless of market conditions.

Tracking can be achieved by trying to hold all of the securities in the index, in the same proportions as the index. Other methods include statistically sampling the market and holding 'representative' securities.

a. A Random Walk Down Wall Street
c. AAB
b. Investment company
d. Index fund

10. In microeconomic theory, an _____ is a graph showing different bundles of goods, each measured as to quantity, between which a consumer is indifferent. That is, at each point on the curve, the consumer has no preference for one bundle over another. In other words, they are all equally preferred. One can equivalently refer to each point on the _____ as rendering the same level of utility (satisfaction) for the consumer.

a. ABN Amro
c. Indifference curve
b. AAB
d. A Random Walk Down Wall Street

Chapter 8. RISKFREE BORROWING AND LENDING

1. In business and accounting, _____s are everything of value that is owned by a person or company. The balance sheet of a firm records the monetary value of the _____s owned by the firm. The two major _____ classes are tangible _____s and intangible _____s.
   a. Accounts payable
   b. EBITDA
   c. Income
   d. Asset

2. In finance, a _____ is a debt security, in which the authorized issuer owes the holders a debt and, depending on the terms of the _____, is obliged to pay interest (the coupon) and/or to repay the principal at a later date, termed maturity.

   Thus a _____ is a loan: the issuer is the borrower, the _____ holder is the lender, and the coupon is the interest. _____s provide the borrower with external funds to finance long-term investments, or, in the case of government _____s, to finance current expenditure.

   a. Convertible bond
   b. Puttable bond
   c. Catastrophe bonds
   d. Bond

3. A _____ is a fungible, negotiable instrument representing financial value. They are broadly categorized into debt securities (such as banknotes, bonds and debentures), and equity securities; e.g., common stocks. The company or other entity issuing the _____ is called the issuer.
   a. Security
   b. Book entry
   c. Tracking stock
   d. Securities lending

4. In finance, the _____ is the global financial market for short-term borrowing and lending. It provides short-term liquidity funding for the global financial system. The _____ is where short-term obligations such as Treasury bills, commercial paper and bankers' acceptances are bought and sold.
   a. Money market
   b. Debt-for-equity swap
   c. Cramdown
   d. Consumer debt

5. In economics, the concept of the _____ refers to the decision-making time frame of a firm in which at least one factor of production is fixed. Costs which are fixed in the _____ have no impact on a firms decisions. For example a firm can raise output by increasing the amount of labour through overtime.
   a. 4-4-5 Calendar
   b. 529 plan
   c. Long-run
   d. Short-run

6. In economics, business, and accounting, a _____ is the value of money that has been used up to produce something, and hence is not available for use anymore. In business, the _____ may be one of acquisition, in which case the amount of money expended to acquire it is counted as _____. In this case, money is the input that is gone in order to acquire the thing.
   a. Marginal cost
   b. Cost
   c. Sliding scale fees
   d. Fixed costs

7. In economics and finance, _____ is the practice of taking advantage of a price differential between two or more markets: striking a combination of matching deals that capitalize upon the imbalance, the profit being the difference between the market prices. When used by academics, an _____ is a transaction that involves no negative cash flow at any probabilistic or temporal state and a positive cash flow in at least one state; in simple terms, a risk-free profit.

a. Issuer
c. Initial margin
b. Efficient-market hypothesis
d. Arbitrage

Chapter 9. THE CAPITAL ASSET PRICING MODEL

1. The term _____ has three unrelated technical definitions, and is also used in a variety of non-technical ways.

   - In financial economics, it refers to any asset used to make money, as opposed to assets used for personal enjoyment or consumption. This is an important distinction because two people can disagree sharply about the value of personal assets, one person might think a sports car is more valuable than a pickup truck, another person might have the opposite taste. But if an asset is held for the purpose of making money, taste has nothing to do with it, only differences of opinion about how much money the asset will produce. With the further assumption that people agree on the probability distribution of future cash flows, it is possible to have an objective _____ pricing model. Even without the assumption of agreement, it is possible to set rational limits on _____ value.
   - In governmental accounting, it is defined as any asset used in operations with an initial useful life extending beyond one reporting period. Generally, government managers have a 'stewardship' duty to maintain _____s under their control. See International Public Sector Accounting Standards for details.
   - In US tax accounting, it is defined as any property other than a list of exceptions. The main exceptions are anything held for sale, and any real estate or depreciable property used in business. Almost everything you own and use for personal purposes, pleasure or investment is a _____. If something is a _____ for tax purposes, gains or losses on sale or disposition are capital gains or capital losses. For individuals, however, capital losses on property held for personal use are generally not deductible. See the IRS publication Tax Facts about Capital Gains and Losses for details.

   A well-known financial accounting textbook advises that the term be avoided except in tax accounting because it is used in so many different senses, not all of them well-defined. For example it is often used as a synonym for fixed assets or for investments in securities.

   A common non-technical usage occurs when people ask that employees or the environment or something else be treated as a _____.

   a. Settlement date
   b. Political risk
   c. Solvency
   d. Capital asset

2. In finance, the _____ is used to determine a theoretically appropriate required rate of return of an asset, if that asset is to be added to an already well-diversified portfolio, given that asset's non-diversifiable risk. The model takes into account the asset's sensitivity to non-diversifiable risk (also known as systemic risk or market risk), often represented by the quantity beta (β) in the financial industry, as well as the expected return of the market and the expected return of a theoretical risk-free asset.

   The model was introduced by Jack Treynor (1961, 1962), William Sharpe (1964), John Lintner (1965a,b) and Jan Mossin (1966) independently, building on the earlier work of Harry Markowitz on diversification and modern portfolio theory.

   a. Capital asset pricing model
   b. Random walk hypothesis
   c. Hull-White model
   d. Cox-Ingersoll-Ross model

3. _____ is the branch of economics that incorporates value judgments (that is, normative judgements) about what the economy ought to be like or what particular policy actions ought to be recommended to achieve a desirable goal. _____ looks at the desirability of certain aspects of the economy. It underlies expressions of support for particular economic policies.

Chapter 9. THE CAPITAL ASSET PRICING MODEL

a. Normative economics
b. Financial risk
c. Fund Accounting
d. Reverse stock split

4. _____ is the branch of economics that concerns the description and explanation of economic phenomena (Wong, 1987, p. 920). It focuses on facts and cause-and-effect relationships and includes the development and testing of economics theories.
   a. 7-Eleven
   b. 529 plan
   c. 4-4-5 Calendar
   d. Positive economics

5. In economics and finance, _____ is the practice of taking advantage of a price differential between two or more markets: striking a combination of matching deals that capitalize upon the imbalance, the profit being the difference between the market prices. When used by academics, an _____ is a transaction that involves no negative cash flow at any probabilistic or temporal state and a positive cash flow in at least one state; in simple terms, a risk-free profit.
   a. Efficient-market hypothesis
   b. Arbitrage
   c. Initial margin
   d. Issuer

6. _____ , in finance, is a general theory of asset pricing, that has become influential in the pricing of stocks.

   _____ holds that the expected return of a financial asset can be modeled as a linear function of various macro-economic factors or theoretical market indices, where sensitivity to changes in each factor is represented by a factor-specific beta coefficient. The model-derived rate of return will then be used to price the asset correctly - the asset price should equal the expected end of period price discounted at the rate implied by model.

   a. ABN Amro
   b. Arbitrage pricing theory
   c. A Random Walk Down Wall Street
   d. AAB

7. In business and accounting, _____s are everything of value that is owned by a person or company. The balance sheet of a firm records the monetary value of the _____s owned by the firm. The two major _____ classes are tangible _____s and intangible _____s.
   a. EBITDA
   b. Accounts payable
   c. Income
   d. Asset

8. In finance, _____ is the process of estimating the potential market value of a financial asset or liability. they can be done on assets (for example, investments in marketable securities such as stocks, options, business enterprises, or intangible assets such as patents and trademarks) or on liabilities (e.g., Bonds issued by a company.) _____s are required in many contexts including investment analysis, capital budgeting, merger and acquisition transactions, financial reporting, taxable events to determine the proper tax liability, and in litigation.
   a. Share
   b. Margin
   c. Procter ' Gamble
   d. Valuation

9. The _____ is the market for securities, where companies and governments can raise longterm funds. The _____ includes the stock market and the bond market. Financial regulators, such as the U.S. Securities and Exchange Commission, oversee the _____s in their designated countries to ensure that investors are protected against fraud.
   a. Spot rate
   b. Capital market
   c. Delta neutral
   d. Forward market

Chapter 9. THE CAPITAL ASSET PRICING MODEL

10. _____ proposes how rational investors will use diversification to optimize their portfolios, and how a risky asset should be priced. The basic concepts of the theory are Markowitz diversification, the efficient frontier, capital asset pricing model, the alpha and beta coefficients, the Capital Market Line and the Securities Market Line.

_____ models an asset's return as a random variable, and models a portfolio as a weighted combination of assets so that the return of a portfolio is the weighted combination of the assets' returns.

a. Consumer basket
b. Modern portfolio theory
c. Market value
d. Payback period

11. A _____ is heuristic and has the following assumptions :

- Rationality of all market actors (Rationality in meaning of the actor's utility maximization)
- No transaction costs (particularly no information costs and no taxes)
- Price taking behavior - there is a sufficiently large number of participants such that no individual can affect the market
- given rare resources
- freedom of decision to do something or to let it be (no external effects)

Share and foreign exchange markets are commonly seen to be the most similar to the _____. The real estate market is an example of a very imperfect market. a free market economy is also related to this _____ system as the public have free will

Other characteristics of a _____ include:-

- No barriers to entry to (or exit from) the market
- Perfect knowledge
- Normal profits

Normal profits are defined as that level of profit which just induces the participants to stay in the market. In other words companies in a _____ pay no dividends, as super-normal profits would induce other participants into the market and drive profits back to the 'normal' level.

This attribute of _____s has profound political and economic implications, as many people assume that the purpose of the market is to enable participants to make profits.

a. 4-4-5 Calendar
b. 529 plan
c. 7-Eleven
d. Perfect market

12. In economics, the _____ asserts that the objective of a firm will be the maximization of its present value, regardless of the preferences of its owners. The theorem therefore separates management's 'productive opportunities' from the entrepreneur's 'market opportunities'.

a. 4-4-5 Calendar
b. 7-Eleven
c. 529 plan
d. Fisher separation theorem

Chapter 9. THE CAPITAL ASSET PRICING MODEL

13. A _____ is a portfolio consisting of a weighted sum of every asset in the market, with weights in the proportions that they exist in the market (with the necessary assumption that these assets are infinitely divisible.)

Neha Tyagi's critique (1977) states that this is only a theoretical concept, as to create a _____ for investment purposes in practice would necessarily include every single possible available asset, including real estate, precious metals, stamp collections, jewelry, and anything with any worth, as the theoretical market being referred to would be the world market. As a result, proxies for the market are used in practice by investors.

- a. Delta neutral
- b. Market price
- c. Central Securities Depository
- d. Market portfolio

14. _____ refers to the stock of skills and knowledge embodied in the ability to perform labor so as to produce economic value. Many early economic theories refer to it simply as labor, one of three factors of production, and consider it to be a fungible resource -- homogeneous and easily interchangeable. Other conceptions of labor dispense with these assumptions.
- a. Market structure
- b. Human capital
- c. Behavioral finance
- d. Mercantilism

15. A _____ is a fungible, negotiable instrument representing financial value. They are broadly categorized into debt securities (such as banknotes, bonds and debentures), and equity securities; e.g., common stocks. The company or other entity issuing the _____ is called the issuer.
- a. Securities lending
- b. Security
- c. Tracking stock
- d. Book entry

16. In Modern Portfolio Theory, the _____ is the graphical representation of the Capital Asset Pricing Model. It displays the expected rate of return for an overall market as a function of systematic (non-diversifiable) risk (beta.)

The Y-Intercept (beta=0) of the _____ is equal to the risk-free interest rate.

- a. Divestment
- b. Certificate in Investment Performance Measurement
- c. Rebalancing
- d. Security market line

17. The _____, in terms of finance and investing, describes how the expected return of a stock or portfolio is correlated to the return of the financial market as a whole.

An asset with a beta of 0 means that its price is not at all correlated with the market; that asset is independent. A positive beta means that the asset generally follows the market.

- a. Current yield
- b. Beta coefficient
- c. Perpetuity
- d. LIBOR market model

18. The _____ is one of several stock market indices, created by nineteenth-century Wall Street Journal editor and Dow Jones ' Company co-founder Charles Dow. Dow compiled the index to gauge the performance of the industrial sector of the American stock market. It is the second-oldest U.S. market index, after the Dow Jones Transportation Average, which Dow also created.

Chapter 9. THE CAPITAL ASSET PRICING MODEL

a. Dow Jones Industrial Average
b. 7-Eleven
c. 4-4-5 Calendar
d. 529 plan

19. In the United States, the Financial Industry Regulatory Authority (FINRA) is a self-regulatory organization (SRO) under the Securities Exchange Act of 1934, successor to the _____.

FINRA is responsible for regulatory oversight of all securities firms that do business with the public; professional training, testing and licensing of registered persons; arbitration and mediation; market regulation by contract for The NASDAQ Stock Market, Inc., the American Stock Exchange LLC, and the International Securities Exchange, LLC; and industry utilities, such as Trade Reporting Facilities and other over-the-counter operations.

a. 7-Eleven
b. NASD
c. 529 plan
d. 4-4-5 Calendar

20. The _____ is an American stock exchange. It is the largest electronic screen-based equity securities trading market in the United States. With approximately 3,200 companies, it has more trading volume per day than any other stock exchange in the world.

a. 7-Eleven
b. Nasdaq
c. 4-4-5 Calendar
d. 529 plan

21. In the United States, the Financial Industry Regulatory Authority (FINRA) is a self-regulatory organization (SRO) under the Securities Exchange Act of 1934, successor to the _____, Inc.

FINRA is responsible for regulatory oversight of all securities firms that do business with the public; professional training, testing and licensing of registered persons; arbitration and mediation; market regulation by contract for The NASDAQ Stock Market, Inc., the American Stock Exchange LLC, and the International Securities Exchange, LLC; and industry utilities, such as Trade Reporting Facilities and other over-the-counter operations.

a. National Association of Securities Dealers
b. 7-Eleven
c. 4-4-5 Calendar
d. 529 plan

22. A _____ is a normalized average (typically a weighted average) of prices for a given class of goods or services in a given region, during a given interval of time. It is a statistic designed to help to compare how these prices, taken as a whole, differ between time periods or geographical locations.

a. Price Index
b. Transfer pricing
c. Price discrimination
d. Discounts and allowances

23. A _____, securities exchange or (in Europe) bourse is a corporation or mutual organization which provides 'trading' facilities for stock brokers and traders, to trade stocks and other securities. _____s also provide facilities for the issue and redemption of securities as well as other financial instruments and capital events including the payment of income and dividends. The securities traded on a _____ include: shares issued by companies, unit trusts and other pooled investment products and bonds.

a. 7-Eleven
b. Stock Exchange
c. 529 plan
d. 4-4-5 Calendar

Chapter 9. THE CAPITAL ASSET PRICING MODEL

24. A _____ is the price of a single share of a no. of saleable stocks of the company. Once the stock is purchased, the owner becomes a shareholder of the company that issued the share.
    a. Trading curb
    b. Whisper numbers
    c. Share price
    d. Stock split

25. In finance, a _____ is a debt security, in which the authorized issuer owes the holders a debt and, depending on the terms of the _____, is obliged to pay interest (the coupon) and/or to repay the principal at a later date, termed maturity.

    Thus a _____ is a loan: the issuer is the borrower, the _____ holder is the lender, and the coupon is the interest. _____s provide the borrower with external funds to finance long-term investments, or, in the case of government _____s, to finance current expenditure.

    a. Convertible bond
    b. Catastrophe bonds
    c. Puttable bond
    d. Bond

26. The _____ is a financial market where participants buy and sell debt securities, usually in the form of bonds. As of 2006, the size of the international _____ is an estimated $45 trillion, of which the size of the outstanding U.S. _____ debt was $25.2 trillion.

    Nearly all of the $923 billion average daily trading volume in the U.S. _____ takes place between broker-dealers and large institutions in a decentralized, over-the-counter market.

    a. 529 plan
    b. Bond market
    c. Fixed income
    d. 4-4-5 Calendar

27. A _____ is a method of measuring a section of the stock market. Many indices are cited by news or financial services firms and are used to benchmark the performance of portfolios such as mutual funds.
    a. Stock market index
    b. Trading curb
    c. Stop order
    d. Program trading

28. _____ is the risk that the value of an investment will decrease due to moves in market factors. The five standard _____ factors are:

    - Equity risk, the risk that stock prices will change.
    - Interest rate risk, the risk that interest rates will change.
    - Currency risk, the risk that foreign exchange rates will change.
    - Commodity risk, the risk that commodity prices (e.g. grains, metals) will change.

    As with other forms of risk, _____ may be measured in a number of ways. Traditionally, this is done using a Value at Risk methodology. Value at risk is well established as a risk management technique, but it contains a number of limiting assumptions that constrain its accuracy.

    a. Tracking error
    b. Transaction risk
    c. Currency risk
    d. Market risk

29. _____ is a measure of the ability of a debtor to pay their debts as and when they fall due. It is usually expressed as a ratio or a percentage of current liabilities.

For a corporation with a published balance sheet there are various ratios used to calculate a measure of liquidity.

a. Operating profit margin
c. Operating leverage
b. Invested capital
d. Accounting liquidity

Chapter 10. FACTOR MODELS

1. In finance, an _____ is the difference between the expected return of a security and the actual return. _____s are sometimes triggered by 'events.' Events can include mergers, dividend announcements, company earning announcements, interest rate increases, lawsuits, etc. all which can contribute to an _____.
   - a. A Random Walk Down Wall Street
   - b. AAB
   - c. ABN Amro
   - d. Abnormal return

2. In probability theory and statistics, _____ is a measure of how much two variables change together (variance is a special case of the _____ when the two variables are identical.)

   If two variables tend to vary together (that is, when one of them is above its expected value, then the other variable tends to be above its expected value too), then the _____ between the two variables will be positive. On the other hand, when one of them is above its expected value the other variable tends to be below its expected value, then the _____ between the two variables will be negative.
   - a. Covariance
   - b. Stratified sampling
   - c. Probability distribution
   - d. Frequency distribution

3. The _____ is the weighted-average most likely outcome in gambling, probability theory, economics or finance.

   In gambling and probability theory, there is usually a discrete set of possible outcomes. In this case, _____ is a measure of the relative balance of win or loss weighted by their chances of occurring.
   - a. ABN Amro
   - b. AAB
   - c. A Random Walk Down Wall Street
   - d. Expected return

4. In probability theory and statistics, the _____ of a random variable, probability distribution averaging the squared distance of its possible values from the expected value (mean.) Whereas the mean is a way to describe the location of a distribution, the _____ is a way to capture its scale or degree of being spread out. The unit of _____ is the square of the unit of the original variable.
   - a. Semivariance
   - b. Variance
   - c. Harmonic mean
   - d. Monte Carlo methods

5. In economics and finance, _____ is the practice of taking advantage of a price differential between two or more markets: striking a combination of matching deals that capitalize upon the imbalance, the profit being the difference between the market prices. When used by academics, an _____ is a transaction that involves no negative cash flow at any probabilistic or temporal state and a positive cash flow in at least one state; in simple terms, a risk-free profit.
   - a. Issuer
   - b. Efficient-market hypothesis
   - c. Initial margin
   - d. Arbitrage

6. _____ in finance is a risk management technique, related to hedging, that mixes a wide variety of investments within a portfolio. Because the fluctuations of a single security have less impact on a diverse portfolio, _____ minimizes the risk from any one investment.

   A simple example of _____ is the following: On a particular island the entire economy consists of two companies: one that sells umbrellas and another that sells sunscreen.

a. 4-4-5 Calendar   b. 529 plan
c. 7-Eleven   d. Diversification

7. A _____ is any actual or hypothesized stock market trend based on the calendar, such as rises and falls associated with particular days of the week or months of the year.

Examples include:

- Halloween indicator (or the 'Sell in May' principle)
- January effect
- Mark Twain effect
- Monday effect
- Weekend effect
- Turn-of-the-Month effect
- Holiday effect

a. 529 plan   b. 7-Eleven
c. 4-4-5 Calendar   d. Calendar effect

Chapter 11. ARBITRAGE PRICING THEORY

1. In economics and finance, _____ is the practice of taking advantage of a price differential between two or more markets: striking a combination of matching deals that capitalize upon the imbalance, the profit being the difference between the market prices. When used by academics, an _____ is a transaction that involves no negative cash flow at any probabilistic or temporal state and a positive cash flow in at least one state; in simple terms, a risk-free profit.
   a. Efficient-market hypothesis
   b. Initial margin
   c. Arbitrage
   d. Issuer

2. _____ , in finance, is a general theory of asset pricing, that has become influential in the pricing of stocks.

   _____ holds that the expected return of a financial asset can be modeled as a linear function of various macro-economic factors or theoretical market indices, where sensitivity to changes in each factor is represented by a factor-specific beta coefficient. The model-derived rate of return will then be used to price the asset correctly - the asset price should equal the expected end of period price discounted at the rate implied by model.

   a. Arbitrage pricing theory
   b. A Random Walk Down Wall Street
   c. ABN Amro
   d. AAB

3. In finance, the _____ is used to determine a theoretically appropriate required rate of return of an asset, if that asset is to be added to an already well-diversified portfolio, given that asset's non-diversifiable risk. The model takes into account the asset's sensitivity to non-diversifiable risk (also known as systemic risk or market risk), often represented by the quantity beta (β) in the financial industry, as well as the expected return of the market and the expected return of a theoretical risk-free asset.

   The model was introduced by Jack Treynor (1961, 1962), William Sharpe (1964), John Lintner (1965a,b) and Jan Mossin (1966) independently, building on the earlier work of Harry Markowitz on diversification and modern portfolio theory.

   a. Cox-Ingersoll-Ross model
   b. Random walk hypothesis
   c. Capital asset pricing model
   d. Hull-White model

4.

   In finance, the _____ can be the expected rate of return above the risk-free interest rate. When measuring risk, a common sense approach is to compare the risk-free return on T-bills and the very risky return on other investments. The difference between these two returns can be interpreted as a measure of the excess return on the average risky asset. This excess return is known as the _____.

   a. Risk adjusted return on capital
   b. Risk premium
   c. Risk aversion
   d. Risk modeling

Chapter 12. TAXES AND INFLATION

1. _____ refers to a tax levied by various jurisdictions on the profits made by companies or associations. It is a tax on the value of the corporation's profits.

The measure of taxable profits varies from country to country.

   a. Proxy fight
   b. Corporate tax
   c. Trade finance
   d. First-mover advantage

2. _____, refers to consumption opportunity gained by an entity within a specified time frame, which is generally expressed in monetary terms. However, for households and individuals, '_____ is the sum of all the wages, salaries, profits, interests payments, rents and other forms of earnings received... in a given period of time.' For firms, _____ generally refers to net-profit: what remains of revenue after expenses have been subtracted.

   a. Income
   b. Accrual
   c. OIBDA
   d. Annual report

3. An _____ is a tax levied on the financial income of people, corporations, or other legal entities. Various _____ systems exist, with varying degrees of tax incidence. Income taxation can be progressive, proportional, or regressive.

   a. AAB
   b. A Random Walk Down Wall Street
   c. Income tax
   d. ABN Amro

4. In finance, a _____ is a debt security, in which the authorized issuer owes the holders a debt and, depending on the terms of the _____, is obliged to pay interest (the coupon) and/or to repay the principal at a later date, termed maturity.

Thus a _____ is a loan: the issuer is the borrower, the _____ holder is the lender, and the coupon is the interest. _____s provide the borrower with external funds to finance long-term investments, or, in the case of government _____s, to finance current expenditure.

   a. Catastrophe bonds
   b. Convertible bond
   c. Puttable bond
   d. Bond

5. _____ is typically a higher ranking stock than voting shares, and its terms are negotiated between the corporation and the investor.

_____ usually carry no voting rights, but may carry superior priority over common stock in the payment of dividends and upon liquidation. _____ may carry a dividend that is paid out prior to any dividends to common stock holders.

   a. Follow-on offering
   b. Trade-off theory
   c. Second lien loan
   d. Preferred stock

6. In business and finance, a _____ (also referred to as equity _____) of stock means a _____ of ownership in a corporation (company.) In the plural, stocks is often used as a synonym for _____s especially in the United States, but it is less commonly used that way outside of North America.

In the United Kingdom, South Africa, and Australia, stock can also refer to completely different financial instruments such as government bonds or, less commonly, to all kinds of marketable securities.

a. Margin
b. Bucket shop
c. Procter ' Gamble
d. Share

7. A _____ is a pool of assets forming an independent legal entity that are bought with the contributions to a pension plan for the exclusive purpose of financing pension plan benefits.

_____s are important shareholders of listed and private companies. They are especially important to the stock market where large institutional investors like the Ontario Teachers' Pension Plan dominate.

a. Limited liability company
b. Leveraged buyout
c. Leverage
d. Pension fund

8. A _____ is a profit that results from investments into a capital asset, such as stocks, bonds or real estate, which exceeds the purchase price. It is the difference between a higher selling price and a lower purchase price, resulting in a financial gain for the seller. Conversely, a capital loss arises if the proceeds from the sale of a capital asset are less than the purchase price.

a. Capital gain
b. Payroll tax
c. Tax brackets
d. Capital gains tax

9. The _____ is an American stock exchange. It is the largest electronic screen-based equity securities trading market in the United States. With approximately 3,200 companies, it has more trading volume per day than any other stock exchange in the world.

a. 7-Eleven
b. 529 plan
c. 4-4-5 Calendar
d. Nasdaq

10. Realization is generally understood in financial circles as the point at which revenue is recognized, typically through a transaction which involves the exchange of an asset, product, or service for cash or its equivalents.

This approach gives the accounting division a strictly objective basis for changing the books. For example, a homeowner may believe that his house has grown in value during a strong market, or fallen in value during a weak market, but until the house is actually sold for a specific price to a specific buyer, the change in value can only be estimated and is considered _____.

a. AAB
b. ABN Amro
c. A Random Walk Down Wall Street
d. Unrealized

11. _____ is a sale of a security (stock, bonds, options) at a loss and repurchasing the same or substantially identical stock soon afterwards. The idea is to make an unrealised loss claimable as a tax deduction, by offsetting against other capital gains in the current or future tax years. The security is repurchased in the hope that it will recover its previous value.

a. Stop-limit order
b. Block premium
c. Wash sale
d. Program trading

12. _____s are full-fledged pension plans for self-employed people in the United States. They are sometimes called HR10 plans and are not Individual Retirement Accounts (IRA.)

Chapter 12. TAXES AND INFLATION

Since a _____ is a full-fledged pension, there is a Keogh for every employer-sponsored pension-plan design.

a. 4-4-5 Calendar
b. 529 plan
c. 7-Eleven
d. Keogh plan

13. _____ is an income tax in the United States that is levied by each individual state. Seven states choose to impose no income tax. These states are Alaska, Florida, Nevada, South Dakota, Texas, Washington, and Wyoming.

a. 529 plan
b. State income tax
c. 7-Eleven
d. 4-4-5 Calendar

14. An _____ is a retirement plan account that provides some tax advantages for retirement savings in the United States.

a. A Random Walk Down Wall Street
b. ABN Amro
c. AAB
d. Individual Retirement Arrangement

15. In economics, _____ is a rise in the general level of prices of goods and services in an economy over a period of time. The term '_____' once referred to increases in the money supply (monetary _____); however, economic debates about the relationship between money supply and price levels have led to its primary use today in describing price _____. _____ can also be described as a decline in the real value of money--a loss of purchasing power in the medium of exchange which is also the monetary unit of account.

a. A Random Walk Down Wall Street
b. AAB
c. ABN Amro
d. Inflation

16. _____ measures the rate of return on the ownership interest (shareholders' equity) of the common stock owners. _____ is viewed as one of the most important financial ratios. It measures a firm's efficiency at generating profits from every dollar of shareholders' equity (also known as net assets or assets minus liabilities.)

a. Return on sales
b. Diluted Earnings Per Share
c. Return of capital
d. Return on equity

17. _____, in bookkeeping, refers to assets, liabilities, income, and expenses recorded on individual pages of the so called book of final entry or ledger. Changes in _____ value are made by chronologically posting debit (DR) and credit (CR) entries to its page. Examples of _____s are cash, _____s receivable, mortgages, loans, land and buildings, common stock, sales, services provided, wages, and payroll overhead.

a. Account
b. Accretion
c. Alpha
d. Option

18. A _____ is a tax charged on capital gains, the profit realized on the sale of a non-inventory asset that was purchased at a lower price. The most common capital gains are realized from the sale of stocks, bonds, precious metals and property. Not all countries implement a _____ and most have different rates of taxation for individuals and corporations.

a. Withholding tax
b. Capital gains tax
c. Tax brackets
d. Tax holiday

Chapter 12. TAXES AND INFLATION

19. A _____ is a measure of the average price of consumer goods and services purchased by households. The _____ can be used to index (i.e., adjust for the effects of inflation) wages, salaries, pensions, or regulated or contracted prices. The _____ is, along with the population census and the National Income and Product Accounts, one of the most closely watched national economic statistics.

   a. Divisia index
   b. Consumer Price Index
   c. 4-4-5 Calendar
   d. 529 plan

20. A _____ is a theoretical price index that measures relative cost of living over time. It is an index that measures differences in the price of goods and services, and allows for substitutions to other items as prices change.

   There are many different methodologies that have been developed to approximate _____es, including methods that allow for substitution among items as relative prices change.

   a. Cost-of-living index
   b. 4-4-5 Calendar
   c. 7-Eleven
   d. 529 plan

21. A _____ is a normalized average (typically a weighted average) of prices for a given class of goods or services in a given region, during a given interval of time. It is a statistic designed to help to compare how these prices, taken as a whole, differ between time periods or geographical locations.

   a. Transfer pricing
   b. Price discrimination
   c. Discounts and allowances
   d. Price Index

22. The _____, in mathematics, is a type of mean or average, which indicates the central tendency or typical value of a set of numbers. It is similar to the arithmetic mean, which is what most people think of with the word 'average,' except that instead of adding the set of numbers and then dividing the sum by the count of numbers in the set, n, the numbers are multiplied and then the nth root of the resulting product is taken.

   For instance, the _____ of two numbers, say 2 and 8, is just the square root (i.e., the second root) of their product, 16, which is 4.

   a. Statistics
   b. Geometric mean
   c. Kurtosis
   d. Standard deviation

23. In statistics, _____ has two related meanings:

   - the arithmetic _____
   - the expected value of a random variable, which is also called the population _____.

   It is sometimes stated that the '_____' is average. This is incorrect if '_____' is taken in the specific sense of 'arithmetic _____' as there are different types of averages: the _____, median, and mode. Other simple statistical analyses use measures of spread, such as range, interquartile range, or standard deviation. For a real-valued random variable X, the _____ is the expectation of X. Note that not every probability distribution has a defined _____; see the Cauchy distribution for an example.

Chapter 12. TAXES AND INFLATION

a. Probability distribution
c. Harmonic mean
b. Mean
d. Sample size

24. _____ is a fee paid on borrowed assets. It is the price paid for the use of borrowed money, or, money earned by deposited funds. Assets that are sometimes lent with _____ include money, shares, consumer goods through hire purchase, major assets such as aircraft, and even entire factories in finance lease arrangements.
   a. AAB
   c. A Random Walk Down Wall Street
   b. Insolvency
   d. Interest

25. An _____ is the price a borrower pays for the use of money they do not own, and the return a lender receives for deferring the use of funds, by lending it to the borrower. _____s are normally expressed as a percentage rate over the period of one year.

   _____s targets are also a vital tool of monetary policy and are used to control variables like investment, inflation, and unemployment.

   a. AAB
   c. Interest rate
   b. ABN Amro
   d. A Random Walk Down Wall Street

26. A _____ is an international bond that is denominated in a currency not native to the country where it is issued. It can be categorised according to the currency in which it is issued. London is one of the centers of the _____ market, but _____s may be traded throughout the world - for example in Singapore or Tokyo.
   a. Interest rate option
   c. Education production function
   b. Economic entity
   d. Eurobond

27. A _____ is a bond issued by a national government denominated in the country's own currency. Bonds issued by national governments in foreign currencies are normally referred to as sovereign bonds. The first ever _____ was issued by the British government in 1693 to raise money to fund a war against France.
   a. Municipal bond
   c. Collateralized debt obligations
   b. Zero-coupon bond
   d. Government bond

28. _____ is a technique to adjust income payments by means of a price index, in order to maintain the purchasing power of the public after inflation.

Applying a cost-of-living escalation COLA clause to a stream of periodic payments protects the real value of those payments and effectively transfers the risk of inflation from the payee to the payor, who must pay more each year to reflect the increases in prices. Thus, inflation _____ is often applied to pension payments, rents and other situations which are not subject to regular re-pricing in the market.

   a. Indexation
   c. A Random Walk Down Wall Street
   b. ABN Amro
   d. AAB

29. In economics, _____ is the removal of intermediaries in a supply chain: 'cutting out the middleman'. Instead of going through traditional distribution channels, which had some type of intermediate (such as a distributor, wholesaler, broker, or agent), companies may now deal with every customer directly, for example via the Internet. One important factor is a drop in the cost of servicing customers directly.

a. 7-Eleven
b. 529 plan
c. Disintermediation
d. 4-4-5 Calendar

30. A _____ refers to any type debt instrument, such as a loan, bond, mortgage that does not have a fixed rate of interest over the life of the instrument. Such debt typically uses an index or other base rate for establishing the interest rate for each relevant period. One of the most common rates to use as the basis for applying interest rates is the London Inter-bank Offered Rate, or LIBOR
   a. Disposal tax effect
   b. Cost of living
   c. Floating interest rate
   d. Foreign exchange hedge

31. A _____ is an exchange of promises between two or more parties to do an act which is enforceable in a court of law. It is where an unqualified offer meets a qualified acceptance and the parties reach Consensus ad Idem. The parties must have the necessary capacity to _____ and the _____ must not be either trifling, indeterminate, impossible or illegal.
   a. 529 plan
   b. Contract
   c. 4-4-5 Calendar
   d. 7-Eleven

32. In economic models, the _____ time frame assumes no fixed factors of production. Firms can enter or leave the marketplace, and the cost (and availability) of land, labor, raw materials, and capital goods can be assumed to vary. In contrast, in the short-run time frame, certain factors are assumed to be fixed, because there is not sufficient time for them to change.
   a. 529 plan
   b. 4-4-5 Calendar
   c. Short-run
   d. Long-run

33. The _____ is a term coined by economists Rajnish Mehra and Edward C. Prescott. It is based on the observation that in order to reconcile the much higher return on equity stock compared to government bonds in the United States, individuals must have implausibly high risk aversion according to standard economics models. Similar situations prevail in many other industrialized countries.
   a. A Random Walk Down Wall Street
   b. AAB
   c. Equity premium puzzle
   d. ABN Amro

34. In economics, the concept of the _____ refers to the decision-making time frame of a firm in which at least one factor of production is fixed. Costs which are fixed in the _____ have no impact on a firms decisions. For example a firm can raise output by increasing the amount of labour through overtime.
   a. 4-4-5 Calendar
   b. Long-run
   c. 529 plan
   d. Short-run

Chapter 13. FIXED-INCOME SECURITIES

1. A _____ is a type of financial intermediary and a type of bank. Commercial banking is also known as business banking. It is a bank that provides checking accounts, savings accounts, and money market accounts and that accepts time deposits.

   a. 7-Eleven
   c. 529 plan
   b. 4-4-5 Calendar
   d. Commercial bank

2. The coupon or _____ of a bond is the amount of interest paid per year expressed as a percentage of the face value of the bond.

   For example if you hold $10,000 nominal of a bond described as a 4.5% loan stock, you will receive $450 in interest each year (probably in two installments of $225 each.)

   Not all bonds have coupons.

   a. Puttable bond
   c. Revenue bonds
   b. Coupon rate
   d. Zero-coupon bond

3. _____ is a type of bank account where the money in the account is legally able to be withdrawn immediately upon demand (or 'at call'.) This type of bank account can also be referred to as a 'cheque' or 'checking' or transactional account.

   This type of bank account, allowing immediate conversion of the account balance into cash or withdrawal to another account, can be contrasted with a time deposit (also known as a certificate of deposit or term deposit), where the funds are not legally available for immediate withdrawal by the depositor.

   a. Synthetic lease
   c. 529 plan
   b. Demand deposit
   d. 4-4-5 Calendar

4. A _____ is an international bond that is denominated in a currency not native to the country where it is issued. It can be categorised according to the currency in which it is issued. London is one of the centers of the _____ market, but _____s may be traded throughout the world - for example in Singapore or Tokyo.

   a. Education production function
   c. Economic entity
   b. Interest rate option
   d. Eurobond

5. _____s are deposits denominated in United States dollars at banks outside the United States, and thus are not under the jurisdiction of the Federal Reserve. Consequently, such deposits are subject to much less regulation than similar deposits within the United States, allowing for higher margins. There is nothing 'European' about _____ deposits; a US dollar-denominated deposit in Tokyo or Caracas would likewise be deemed _____ deposits.

   a. A Random Walk Down Wall Street
   c. ABN Amro
   b. AAB
   d. Eurodollar

6. _____ refers to any type of investment that yields a regular (or fixed) return.

Chapter 13. FIXED-INCOME SECURITIES

For example, if you lend money to a borrower and the borrower has to pay interest once a month, you have been issued a fixed-income security. When a company does this, it is often called a bond or corporate bank debt (although preferred stock is also sometimes considered to be _____).

a. 4-4-5 Calendar
b. 529 plan
c. Bond market
d. Fixed income

7. _____ is a life of security. It may also refer to the final payment date of a loan or other financial instrument, at which point all remaining interest and principal is due to be paid.

1, 3, 6 months _____ band can be calculated by using 30-day per month periods.

a. False billing
b. Maturity
c. Primary market
d. Replacement cost

8. A _____ is a fungible, negotiable instrument representing financial value. They are broadly categorized into debt securities (such as banknotes, bonds and debentures), and equity securities; e.g., common stocks. The company or other entity issuing the _____ is called the issuer.

a. Book entry
b. Tracking stock
c. Securities lending
d. Security

9. A _____ is a measure of the average price of consumer goods and services purchased by households. The _____ can be used to index (i.e., adjust for the effects of inflation) wages, salaries, pensions, or regulated or contracted prices. The _____ is, along with the population census and the National Income and Product Accounts, one of the most closely watched national economic statistics.

a. 529 plan
b. 4-4-5 Calendar
c. Divisia index
d. Consumer price index

10. A _____ s a time deposit, a financial product commonly offered to consumers by banks, thrift institutions, and credit unions.

They are similar to savings accounts in that they are insured and thus virtually risk-free; they are 'money in the bank'. They are different from savings accounts in that they have a specific, fixed term (often three months, six months, or one to five years), and, usually, a fixed interest rate.

a. Reserve requirement
b. Certificate of deposit
c. Variable rate mortgage
d. Time deposit

11. The institution most often referenced by the word '_____' is a public or publicly traded _____, the shares of which are traded on a public stock exchange (e.g., the New York Stock Exchange or Nasdaq in the United States) where shares of stock of _____s are bought and sold by and to the general public. Most of the largest businesses in the world are publicly traded _____s. However, the majority of _____s are said to be closely held, privately held or close _____s, meaning that no ready market exists for the trading of shares.

Chapter 13. FIXED-INCOME SECURITIES

a. Depository Trust Company
c. Protect
b. Federal Home Loan Mortgage Corporation
d. Corporation

12. _____ is the provision of resources (such as granting a loan) by one party to another party where that second party does not reimburse the first party immediately, thereby generating a debt, and instead arranges either to repay or return those resources (or material(s) of equal value) at a later date. The first party is called a creditor, also known as a lender, while the second party is called a debtor, also known as a borrower.

Movements of financial capital are normally dependent on either _____ or equity transfers.

a. Credit
c. Comparable
b. Warrant
d. Clearing house

13. A _____ is a cooperative financial institution that is owned and controlled by its members, and operated for the purpose of promoting thrift, providing credit at reasonable rates, and providing other financial services to its members. Many _____s exist to further community development or sustainable international development on a local level. Worldwide, _____ systems vary significantly in terms of total system assets and average institution asset size since _____s exist in a wide range of sizes, ranging from volunteer operations with a handful of members to institutions with several billion dollars in assets and hundreds of thousands of members.

a. Credit Union Service Organization
c. Corporate credit union
b. Fi-linx
d. Credit union

14. Explicit _____ is a measure implemented in many countries to protect bank depositors, in full or in part, from losses caused by a bank's inability to pay its debts when due. _____ systems are one component of a financial system safety net that promotes financial stability.

a. Reserve requirement
c. Banking panic
b. Time deposit
d. Deposit Insurance

15. The _____ is a United States government corporation created by the Glass-Steagall Act of 1933. It provides deposit insurance, which guarantees the safety of checking and savings deposits in member banks, currently up to $250,000 per depositor per bank. Insured deposits are backed by the full faith and credit of the United States.

a. FASB
c. Ford Foundation
b. NYSE Group
d. Federal Deposit Insurance Corporation

16. A _____ is a normalized average (typically a weighted average) of prices for a given class of goods or services in a given region, during a given interval of time. It is a statistic designed to help to compare how these prices, taken as a whole, differ between time periods or geographical locations.

a. Discounts and allowances
c. Price discrimination
b. Transfer pricing
d. Price Index

17. A _____ is a money deposit at a banking institution that cannot be withdrawn for a certain 'term' or period of time. When the term is over it can be withdrawn or it can be held for another term. Generally speaking, the longer the term the better the yield on the money.

a. Private money
c. Basel Accord
b. Certificate of deposit
d. Time deposit

18. In the global money market, _____ is an unsecured promissory note with a fixed maturity of one to 270 days. _____ is a money-market security issued (sold) by large banks and corporations to get money to meet short term debt obligations (for example, payroll), and is only backed by an issuing bank or corporation's promise to pay the face amount on the maturity date specified on the note. Since it is not backed by collateral, only firms with excellent credit ratings from a recognized rating agency will be able to sell their _____ at a reasonable price.

   a. Financial distress
   b. Trade-off theory
   c. Commercial paper
   d. Book building

19. In finance, the _____ is the global financial market for short-term borrowing and lending. It provides short-term liquidity funding for the global financial system. The _____ is where short-term obligations such as Treasury bills, commercial paper and bankers' acceptances are bought and sold.

   a. Cramdown
   b. Consumer debt
   c. Money market
   d. Debt-for-equity swap

20. A _____ is a financial institution that specializes in accepting savings deposits and making mortgage and other loans. The S'L or thrift term is mainly used in the United States; similar institutions in the United Kingdom, Ireland and some Commonwealth countries include building societies and trustee savings banks.

They are often mutually held, meaning that the depositors and borrowers are members with voting rights, and have the ability to direct the financial and managerial goals of the organization, not unlike the polyholders of a mutual insurance company.

   a. Mutual fund
   b. Net asset value
   c. Person-to-person lending
   d. Savings and loan association

21. A '_____' is a 'Charge' that is paid to obtain the right to delay a payment. Essentially, the payer purchases the right to make a given payment in the future instead of in the Present. The '_____', or 'Charge' that must be paid to delay the payment, is simply the difference between what the payment amount would be if it were paid in the present and what the payment amount would be paid if it were paid in the future.

   a. Risk modeling
   b. Value at risk
   c. Risk aversion
   d. Discount

22. _____ is the term used to describe deposits residing in banks that are located outside the borders of the country that issues the currency the deposit is denominated in. For example a deposit denominated in US dollars residing in a Japanese bank is a _____ deposit, or more specifically a Eurodollar deposit.

Key points are the location of the bank and the denomination of the currency, not the nationality of the bank or the owner of the deposit/loan.

   a. Eurocurrency
   b. A Random Walk Down Wall Street
   c. ABN Amro
   d. AAB

23. The official bank rate has existing in various forms since 1694 and has ranged from 0.5% to 17%. The name of this key interest rate has changed over the years. The current name 'Official Bank Rate' was introduced in 2006 and replaced the previous title '_____' (repo is short for repurchase agreement) in 1997.

Chapter 13. FIXED-INCOME SECURITIES

a. London Interbank Offered Rate
b. London Interbank Bid Rate
c. Cash accumulation equation
d. Repo rate

24. A _____ allows a borrower to use a financial security as collateral for a cash loan at a fixed rate of interest. In a repo, the borrower agrees to immediately sell a security to a lender and also agrees to buy the same security from the lender at a fixed price at some later date. A repo is equivalent to a cash transaction combined with a forward contract.
a. Contango
b. Repurchase agreement
c. Volatility arbitrage
d. Total return swap

25. _____ is that which is owed; usually referencing assets owed, but the term can cover other obligations. In the case of assets, _____ is a means of using future purchasing power in the present before a summation has been earned. Some companies and corporations use _____ as a part of their overall corporate finance strategy.
a. Partial Payment
b. Credit cycle
c. Cross-collateralization
d. Debt

26. _____ are securities that can be easily converted into cash. Such securities will generally have highly liquid markets allowing the security to be sold at a reasonable price very quickly. This is a usual feature in real estate.
a. Book entry
b. Securities lending
c. Marketable
d. Tracking stock

27. _____ occurs when an entity that has issued callable bonds calls those debt securities from the debt holders with the express purpose of reissuing new debt at a lower coupon rate. In essence, the issue of new, lower-interest debt allows the company to prematurely refund the older, higher-interest debt.

On the contrary, NonRefundable Bonds may be callable but they cannot be re-issued with a lower coupon rate.

a. Market neutral
b. Systematic risk
c. No-arbitrage bounds
d. Refunding

28. _____ mature in one year or less. Like zero-coupon bonds, they do not pay interest prior to maturity; instead they are sold at a discount of the par value to create a positive yield to maturity. Many regard _____ as the least risky investment available to U.S. investors.
a. Treasury securities
b. Treasury Inflation Protected Securities
c. 4-4-5 Calendar
d. Treasury bills

29. _____ are government bonds issued by the United States Department of the Treasury through the Bureau of the Public Debt. They are the debt financing instruments of the U.S. Federal government, and they are often referred to simply as Treasuries or Treasurys. There are four types of marketable _____: Treasury bills, Treasury notes, Treasury bonds, and Treasury Inflation Protected Securities (TIPS.)
a. Treasury Inflation Protected Securities
b. 4-4-5 Calendar
c. Treasury Inflation-Protected Securities
d. Treasury securities

30. In finance, the term _____ describes the amount in cash that returns to the owners of a security. Normally it does not include the price variations, at the difference of the total return. _____ applies to various stated rates of return on stocks (common and preferred, and convertible), fixed income instruments (bonds, notes, bills, strips, zero coupon), and some other investment type insurance products (e.g. annuities.)

Chapter 13. FIXED-INCOME SECURITIES

a. Macaulay duration
c. Yield

b. Yield to maturity
d. 4-4-5 Calendar

31. In finance, a _____ is a debt security, in which the authorized issuer owes the holders a debt and, depending on the terms of the _____, is obliged to pay interest (the coupon) and/or to repay the principal at a later date, termed maturity.

Thus a _____ is a loan: the issuer is the borrower, the _____ holder is the lender, and the coupon is the interest. _____s provide the borrower with external funds to finance long-term investments, or, in the case of government _____s, to finance current expenditure.

a. Puttable bond
c. Catastrophe bonds

b. Bond
d. Convertible bond

32. In finance, _____ is the interest that has accumulated since the principal investment, or since the previous interest payment if there has been one already. For a financial instrument such as a bond, interest is calculated and paid in set intervals.

The primary formula for calculating the interest accrued in a given period is:

$$I_A = T \times P \times R$$

where I_A is the _____, T is the fraction of the year, P is the principal, and R is the annualized interest rate.

a. AAB
c. ABN Amro

b. A Random Walk Down Wall Street
d. Accrued interest

33. A _____ is a government debt issued by the United States Department of the Treasury through the Bureau of the Public Debt. They are the debt financing instruments of the United States Federal government, and they are often referred to simply as Treasuries. There are four types of marketable treasury securities: Treasury bills, Treasury notes, Treasury bonds, and Treasury Inflation Protected Securities (TIPS.)

a. United States Treasury security
c. OTC Bulletin Board

b. Insolvency
d. International trade

34. _____ is a fee paid on borrowed assets. It is the price paid for the use of borrowed money, or, money earned by deposited funds. Assets that are sometimes lent with _____ include money, shares, consumer goods through hire purchase, major assets such as aircraft, and even entire factories in finance lease arrangements.

a. A Random Walk Down Wall Street
c. Interest

b. Insolvency
d. AAB

35. A _____ is a bond bought at a price lower than its face value, with the face value repaid at the time of maturity. It does not make periodic interest payments, or have so-called 'coupons,' hence the term _____. Investors earn return from the compounded interest all paid at maturity plus the difference between the discounted price of the bond and its par value.

Chapter 13. FIXED-INCOME SECURITIES

a. Zero-coupon bond
c. Clean price
b. Bond fund
d. Corporate bond

36. The _____ (NYSE: FNM), commonly known as Fannie Mae, is a stockholder-owned corporation chartered by Congress in 1968 as a government sponsored enterprise (GSE), but founded in 1938 during the Great Depression. The corporation's purpose is to purchase and securitize mortgages in order to ensure that funds are consistently available to the institutions that lend money to home buyers.

On September 7, 2008, James Lockhart, director of the Federal Housing Finance Agency (FHFA), announced that Fannie Mae and Freddie Mac were being placed into conservatorship of the FHFA.

a. The Depository Trust ' Clearing Corporation
c. Federal National Mortgage Association
b. General partnership
d. SPDR

37. The _____ provide stable, on-demand, low-cost funding to American financial institutions for home mortgage loans, small business, rural, agricultural, and economic development lending. With their members, the _____ank System represents the largest collective source of home mortgage and community credit in the United States. The banks do not provide loans directly to individuals, only to other banks.

a. 4-4-5 Calendar
c. 529 plan
b. 7-Eleven
d. Federal Home Loan Banks

38. The _____ (NYSE: FRE) is an insolvent government sponsored enterprise (GSE) of the United States federal government.

The _____ was created in 1970 to expand the secondary market for mortgages in the US. Along with other GSEs, Freddie Mac buys mortgages on the secondary market, pools them, and sells them as mortgage-backed securities to investors on the open market.

a. Governmental Accounting Standards Board
c. Federal Home Loan Mortgage Corporation
b. Public company
d. The Depository Trust ' Clearing Corporation

39. The _____ is a U.S. government-owned corporation within the Department of Housing and Urban Development

Ginnie Mae provides guarantees on mortgage-backed securities backed by federally insured or guaranteed loans, mainly loans issued by the Federal Housing Administration, Department of Veterans Affairs, Rural Housing Service, and Office of Public and Indian Housing. Ginnie Mae securities are the only MBS that are guaranteed by the United States government.

a. GNMA
c. Cash budget
b. Certified Emission Reductions
d. Case-Shiller Home Price Indices

40. The _____ is a U.S. government-owned corporation within the Department of Housing and Urban Development

Chapter 13. FIXED-INCOME SECURITIES

Ginnie Mae provides guarantees on mortgage-backed securities backed by federally insured or guaranteed loans, mainly loans issued by the Federal Housing Administration, Department of Veterans Affairs, Rural Housing Service, and Office of Public and Indian Housing. Ginnie Mae securities are the only MBS that are guaranteed by the United States government.

   a. 4-4-5 Calendar
   b. Jumbo mortgage
   c. Graduated payment mortgage
   d. Government National Mortgage Association

41. In finance, 'participation' is an ownership interest in a mortgage or other loan. In particular, _____ is a cooperation of multiple lenders to issue a loan (known as participation loan) to one borrower. This is usually done in order to reduce individual risks of the lenders.
   a. Short positions
   b. Loan participation
   c. Doctrine of the Proper Law
   d. Securitization

42. _____ is early repayment of a loan by a borrower.

In the case of a mortgage-backed security (MBS), _____ is perceived as a risk, because mortgage debts are often paid off early in order to incur lower total interest payments through cheaper refinancing. The new financing may be cheaper because the borrower's credit rating has improved or because interest rates are lower, but in either case, the payments that would have been made to the MBS investor would be above market rates.

   a. Prepayment
   b. Retention ratio
   c. Disposal tax effect
   d. Bankruptcy remote

43. A _____ is a financial debt vehicle that was first created in June 1983 by investment banks Salomon Brothers and First Boston for Freddie Mac. (The First Boston team was led by Dexter Senft.) Legally, a _____ is a special purpose entity that is wholly separate from the institution(s) that create it.
   a. 4-4-5 Calendar
   b. Tranche
   c. Yield curve spread
   d. Collateralized mortgage obligation

44. In the United States, a _____ is a bond issued by a city or other local government, or their agencies. Potential issuers of these bonds include cities, counties, redevelopment agencies, school districts, publicly owned airports and seaports, and any other governmental entity (or group of governments) below the state level. They may be general obligations of the issuer or secured by specified revenues.
   a. Puttable bond
   b. Premium bond
   c. Senior debt
   d. Municipal bond

45. _____ is the standard framework of guidelines for financial accounting used in the United States of America. It includes the standards, conventions, and rules accountants follow in recording and summarizing transactions, and in the preparation of financial statements. _____ are now issued by the Financial Accounting Standards Board (FASB).
   a. Net income
   b. Depreciation
   c. Revenue
   d. Generally Accepted Accounting Principles

46. A _____ is a legal pledge in United States municipal finance, in which an entity pledges its full faith and credit to repay its debt, typically a _____ bond.

Chapter 13. FIXED-INCOME SECURITIES

a. Letter of credit

b. Financial Institutions Reform Recovery and Enforcement Act

c. Covenant

d. General obligation

47. In business, _____ is income that a company receives from its normal business activities, usually from the sale of goods and services to customers. Some companies also receive _____ from interest, dividends or royalties paid to them by other companies. _____ may refer to business income in general, or it may refer to the amount, in a monetary unit, received during a period of time, as in 'Last year, Company X had _____ of $32 million.'

In many countries, including the UK, _____ is referred to as turnover.

a. Matching principle
c. Revenue

b. Bottom line
d. Furniture, Fixtures and Equipment

48. _____ are bonds issued by governments, authorities, or public benefit corporations that are guaranteed by the revenue flow of the issuing agency.

The Supreme Court decision of Pollock versus Farmer's Loan and Trust Company of 1895 initiated a wave or series of innovations for the financial services community in both tax-treatment and regulation from government. This specific case, according to a leading investment bank's research, resulted in the 'intergovernmental tax immunity doctrine,' ultimately leading to 'tax-free status.' Municipal bonds are generally exempt from federal tax on their interest payments (not capital gains.)

a. Gilts
c. Callable bond

b. Private activity bond
d. Revenue bonds

49. A _____ is a bond issued by a corporation. The term is usually applied to longer-term debt instruments, generally with a maturity date falling at least a year after their issue date. (The term 'commercial paper' is sometimes used for instruments with a shorter maturity.)

a. Corporate bond
c. Brady bonds

b. Serial bond
d. Government bond

50. _____s are financial bonds that mature in installments over a period of time. In effect, a $100,000, 5-year _____ would mature in a $20,000 annuity over a 5-year interval. Bond issues consisting of a series of blocks of securities maturing in sequence, the coupon rate can be different.

a. Bond fund
c. Serial bond

b. Brady bonds
d. Callable bond

51. A _____ is a fund established by a government agency or business for the purpose of reducing debt.

The _____ was first used in Great Britain in the 18th century to reduce national debt. While used by Robert Walpole in 1716 and effectively in the 1720s and early 1730s, it originated in the commercial tax syndicates of the Italian peninsula of the 14th century to retire redeemable public debt of those cities.

Chapter 13. FIXED-INCOME SECURITIES

a. Security interest
b. Debtor
c. Modern portfolio theory
d. Sinking fund

52. _____, refers to consumption opportunity gained by an entity within a specified time frame, which is generally expressed in monetary terms. However, for households and individuals, '_____ is the sum of all the wages, salaries, profits, interests payments, rents and other forms of earnings received... in a given period of time.' For firms, _____ generally refers to net-profit: what remains of revenue after expenses have been subtracted.
   a. Annual report
   b. Accrual
   c. Income
   d. OIBDA

53. In lending agreements, _____ is a borrower's pledge of specific property to a lender, to secure repayment of a loan. The _____ serves as protection for a lender against a borrower's risk of default - that is, a borrower failing to pay the principal and interest under the terms of a loan obligation. If a borrower does default on a loan (due to insolvency or other event), that borrower forfeits (gives up) the property pledged as _____ _ollateral_ - and the lender then becomes the owner of the _____.
   a. Nominal value
   b. Collateral
   c. Future-oriented
   d. Refinancing risk

54. A _____ is defined as a certificate of agreement of loans which is given under the company's stamp and carries an undertaking that the _____ holder will get a fixed return (fixed on the basis of interest rates) and the principal amount whenever the _____ matures.

In finance, a _____ is a long-term debt instrument used by governments and large companies to obtain funds. It is defined as 'a debt secured only by the debtor's earning power, not by a lien on any specific asset.' It is similar to a bond except the securitization conditions are different.

   a. Collateral Management
   b. Collection agency
   c. Partial Payment
   d. Debenture

55. An _____ is a security whose value and income payments are derived from and collateralized (or 'backed') by a specified pool of underlying assets. The pool of assets is typically a group of small and illiquid assets that are unable to be sold individually. Pooling the assets allows them to be sold to general investors, a process called securitization, and allows the risk of investing in the underlying assets to be diversified because each security will represent a fraction of the total value of the diverse pool of underlying assets.
   a. A Random Walk Down Wall Street
   b. ABN Amro
   c. Asset-backed security
   d. AAB

56. In finance, a _____ is a type of bond that can be converted into shares of stock in the issuing company, usually at some pre-announced ratio. It is a hybrid security with debt- and equity-like features. Although it typically has a low coupon rate, the holder is compensated with the ability to convert the bond to common stock, usually at a substantial discount to the stock's market value.
   a. Bond fund
   b. Gilts
   c. Corporate bond
   d. Convertible bond

57. _____ is a combination of straight bond and embedded put option. The holder of the _____ has the right, but not the obligation, to demand early repayment of the principal. The put option is usually exercisable on specified dates.

Chapter 13. FIXED-INCOME SECURITIES

a. Puttable bond
b. Convertible bond
c. Brady bonds
d. Callable bond

58. In financial accounting, _____s are precautions for which the amount or probability of occurrence are not known. Typical examples are _____s for warranty costs and _____ for taxes the term reserve is used instead of term _____; such a use, however, is inconsistent with the terminology suggested by International Accounting Standards Board.
a. Petty cash
b. Provision
c. Money measurement concept
d. Momentum Accounting and Triple-Entry Bookkeeping

59. _____ is a legally declared inability or impairment of ability of an individual or organization to pay their creditors. Creditors may file a _____ petition against a debtor ('involuntary _____') in an effort to recoup a portion of what they are owed or initiate a restructuring. In the majority of cases, however, _____ is initiated by the debtor (a 'voluntary _____' that is filed by the bankrupt individual or organization.)
a. Bankruptcy
b. 529 plan
c. 4-4-5 Calendar
d. Debt settlement

60. In the United States, a _____ is an offering of securities that are not registered with the Securities and Exchange Commission (SEC.) Such offerings exploit an exemption offered by the Securities Act of 1933 that comes with several restrictions, including a prohibition against general solicitation. This exemption allows companies to avoid quarterly reporting requirements and many of the legal liabilities associated with the Sarbanes-Oxley Act.
a. Private placement
b. 529 plan
c. 7-Eleven
d. 4-4-5 Calendar

61. In law, _____ refers to the process by which a company (or part of a company) is brought to an end, and the assets and property of the company redistributed. _____ can also be referred to as winding-up or dissolution, although dissolution technically refers to the last stage of _____. The process of _____ also arises when customs, an authority or agency in a country responsible for collecting and safeguarding customs duties, determines the final computation or ascertainment of the duties or drawback accruing on an entry.
a. 529 plan
b. 4-4-5 Calendar
c. Debt settlement
d. Liquidation

62. _____ are securities of companies or government entities that are either already in default, under bankruptcy protection, or in distress and heading toward such a condition. The most common _____ are bonds and bank debt. While there is no precise definition, fixed income instruments with a yield to maturity in excess of 1000 basis points over the risk-free rate of return (e.g. Treasuries) are commonly thought of as being distressed.
a. 4-4-5 Calendar
b. Distressed securities
c. 529 plan
d. 7-Eleven

63. In the United States, the Financial Industry Regulatory Authority (FINRA) is a self-regulatory organization (SRO) under the Securities Exchange Act of 1934, successor to the _____, Inc.

Chapter 13. FIXED-INCOME SECURITIES

FINRA is responsible for regulatory oversight of all securities firms that do business with the public; professional training, testing and licensing of registered persons; arbitration and mediation; market regulation by contract for The NASDAQ Stock Market, Inc., the American Stock Exchange LLC, and the International Securities Exchange, LLC; and industry utilities, such as Trade Reporting Facilities and other over-the-counter operations.

a. 529 plan
b. 4-4-5 Calendar
c. National Association of Securities Dealers
d. 7-Eleven

64. In business and finance, a _____ (also referred to as equity _____) of stock means a _____ of ownership in a corporation (company.) In the plural, stocks is often used as a synonym for _____s especially in the United States, but it is less commonly used that way outside of North America.

In the United Kingdom, South Africa, and Australia, stock can also refer to completely different financial instruments such as government bonds or, less commonly, to all kinds of marketable securities.

a. Margin
b. Bucket shop
c. Procter ' Gamble
d. Share

65. A _____ is a type of auction where the auctioneer begins with a high asking price which is lowered until some participant is willing to accept the auctioneer's price, or a predetermined reserve price (the seller's minimum acceptable price) is reached. The winning participant pays the last announced price. This is also known as a 'clock auction' or an open-outcry descending-price auction.

a. 4-4-5 Calendar
b. 529 plan
c. 7-Eleven
d. Dutch auction

66. _____ is capital stock which provides a specific dividend that is paid before any dividends are paid to common stock holders, and which takes precedence over common stock in the event of a liquidation. This form of financing is used by private equity investors and venture capital firms. Holders of _____ get both their money back (with interest) and the money that is distributable with respect to the percentage of common shares into which their preferred stock can convert.

a. Shareholder value
b. Preferred stock
c. Cash is king
d. Participating preferred stock

67. _____ is typically a higher ranking stock than voting shares, and its terms are negotiated between the corporation and the investor.

_____ usually carry no voting rights, but may carry superior priority over common stock in the payment of dividends and upon liquidation. _____ may carry a dividend that is paid out prior to any dividends to common stock holders.

a. Second lien loan
b. Follow-on offering
c. Preferred stock
d. Trade-off theory

Chapter 14. BOND ANALYSIS

1. In finance, a _____ is a debt security, in which the authorized issuer owes the holders a debt and, depending on the terms of the _____, is obliged to pay interest (the coupon) and/or to repay the principal at a later date, termed maturity.

Thus a _____ is a loan: the issuer is the borrower, the _____ holder is the lender, and the coupon is the interest. _____s provide the borrower with external funds to finance long-term investments, or, in the case of government _____s, to finance current expenditure.

   a. Bond
   c. Puttable bond
   b. Convertible bond
   d. Catastrophe bonds

2. The _____ is a capital budgeting metric used by firms to decide whether they should make investments. It is an indicator of the efficiency or quality of an investment, as opposed to net present value (NPV), which indicates value or magnitude.

The IRR is the annualized effective compounded return rate which can be earned on the invested capital, i.e., the yield on the investment.

   a. A Random Walk Down Wall Street
   c. Internal rate of return
   b. AAB
   d. ABN Amro

3. _____ is equal to the income that a firm has after subtracting costs and expenses from the total revenue. _____ can be distributed among holders of common stock as a dividend or held by the firm as retained earnings. _____ is an accounting term; in some countries (such as the UK) profit is the usual term.
   a. Write-off
   c. Historical cost
   b. Furniture, Fixtures and Equipment
   d. Net income

4. The _____ or redemption yield is the yield promised to the bondholder on the assumption that the bond or other fixed-interest security such as gilts will be held to maturity, that all coupon and principal payments will be made and coupon payments are reinvested at the bond's promised yield at the same rate as invested. It is a measure of the return of the bond. This technique in theory allows investors to calculate the fair value of different financial instruments.
   a. 4-4-5 Calendar
   c. Yield
   b. Macaulay duration
   d. Yield to maturity

5. _____, refers to consumption opportunity gained by an entity within a specified time frame, which is generally expressed in monetary terms. However, for households and individuals, '_____ is the sum of all the wages, salaries, profits, interests payments, rents and other forms of earnings received... in a given period of time.' For firms, _____ generally refers to net-profit: what remains of revenue after expenses have been subtracted.
   a. Annual report
   c. OIBDA
   b. Income
   d. Accrual

6. In finance, _____, also known as return on investment is the ratio of money gained or lost on an investment relative to the amount of money invested. The amount of money gained or lost may be referred to as interest, profit/loss, gain/loss, or net income/loss. The money invested may be referred to as the asset, capital, principal, or the cost basis of the investment.
   a. Rate of return
   c. Composiition of Creditors
   b. Stock or scrip dividends
   d. Doctrine of the Proper Law

Chapter 14. BOND ANALYSIS

7. In finance, _____ refers to the value of a security which is intrinsic to or contained in the security itself. It is also frequently called fundamental value. It is ordinarily calculated by summing the future income generated by the asset, and discounting it to the present value.
   a. Amortization
   b. Intrinsic value
   c. Alpha
   d. Accretion

8. In finance, _____ is the process of estimating the potential market value of a financial asset or liability. they can be done on assets (for example, investments in marketable securities such as stocks, options, business enterprises, or intangible assets such as patents and trademarks) or on liabilities (e.g., Bonds issued by a company.) _____s are required in many contexts including investment analysis, capital budgeting, merger and acquisition transactions, financial reporting, taxable events to determine the proper tax liability, and in litigation.
   a. Share
   b. Margin
   c. Valuation
   d. Procter ' Gamble

9. In finance, the term _____ describes the amount in cash that returns to the owners of a security. Normally it does not include the price variations, at the difference of the total return. _____ applies to various stated rates of return on stocks (common and preferred, and convertible), fixed income instruments (bonds, notes, bills, strips, zero coupon), and some other investment type insurance products (e.g. annuities.)
   a. Yield
   b. 4-4-5 Calendar
   c. Yield to maturity
   d. Macaulay duration

10. A _____ is a unit that is equal to 1/100th of a percentage point. It is frequently used to express percentage point changes of less than 1%. It avoids the ambiguity between relative and absolute discussions about rates.
    a. Basis point
    b. Bond market
    c. 529 plan
    d. 4-4-5 Calendar

11. The coupon or _____ of a bond is the amount of interest paid per year expressed as a percentage of the face value of the bond.

For example if you hold $10,000 nominal of a bond described as a 4.5% loan stock, you will receive $450 in interest each year (probably in two installments of $225 each.)

Not all bonds have coupons.

   a. Revenue bonds
   b. Puttable bond
   c. Coupon rate
   d. Zero-coupon bond

12. _____ is the long dimension of any object. The _____ of a thing is the distance between its ends, its linear extent as measured from end to end. This may be distinguished from height, which is vertical extent, and width or breadth, which are the distance from side to side, measuring across the object at right angles to the _____.
    a. Length
    b. 4-4-5 Calendar
    c. 7-Eleven
    d. 529 plan

13. In finance, the _____ is the difference between the quoted rates of return on two different investments, usually of different credit quality.

Chapter 14. BOND ANALYSIS

It is a compound of yield and spread.

The '_____ of X over Y' is simply the percentage return on investment (ROI) from financial instrument X minus the percentage return on investment from financial instrument Y (per annum.)

a. Debtor-in-possession financing
b. Duty of loyalty
c. Portfolio insurance
d. Yield spread

14. _____ is a life of security. It may also refer to the final payment date of a loan or other financial instrument, at which point all remaining interest and principal is due to be paid.

1, 3, 6 months _____ band can be calculated by using 30-day per month periods.

a. Replacement cost
b. Primary market
c. Maturity
d. False billing

15. _____ is a type of bond that allows the issuer of the bond to retain the privilege of redeeming the bond at some point before the bond reaches the date of maturity. In other words, on the call dates, the issuer has the right, but not the obligation, to buy back the bonds from the bond holders at the call price. Technically speaking, the bonds are not really bought and held by the issuer but cancelled immediately.

a. Bond fund
b. Callable bond
c. Gilts
d. Coupon rate

16. _____ is a combination of straight bond and embedded put option. The holder of the _____ has the right, but not the obligation, to demand early repayment of the principal. The put option is usually exercisable on specified dates.

a. Callable bond
b. Convertible bond
c. Brady bonds
d. Puttable bond

17. In financial accounting, _____s are precautions for which the amount or probability of occurrence are not known. Typical examples are _____s for warranty costs and _____ for taxes the term reserve is used instead of term _____; such a use, however, is inconsistent with the terminology suggested by International Accounting Standards Board.

a. Petty cash
b. Momentum Accounting and Triple-Entry Bookkeeping
c. Provision
d. Money measurement concept

18. A _____ is an international bond that is denominated in a currency not native to the country where it is issued. It can be categorised according to the currency in which it is issued. London is one of the centers of the _____ market, but _____s may be traded throughout the world - for example in Singapore or Tokyo.

a. Education production function
b. Interest rate option
c. Economic entity
d. Eurobond

Chapter 14. BOND ANALYSIS

19. A '_____' is a 'Charge' that is paid to obtain the right to delay a payment. Essentially, the payer purchases the right to make a given payment in the future instead of in the Present. The '_____', or 'Charge' that must be paid to delay the payment, is simply the difference between what the payment amount would be if it were paid in the present and what the payment amount would be paid if it were paid in the future.

   a. Value at risk
   b. Risk aversion
   c. Risk modeling
   d. Discount

20. A _____ is a bond bought at a price lower than its face value, with the face value repaid at the time of maturity. It does not make periodic interest payments, or so-called 'coupons,' hence the term zero-coupon bond. Investors earn return from the compounded interest all paid at maturity plus the difference between the discounted price of the bond and its par value.

   a. Municipal bond
   b. Zero coupon bond
   c. Callable bond
   d. Bowie bonds

21. A _____ or market-based mechanism is any of a wide variety of ways to match up buyers and sellers.

   An example of a _____ uses announced bid and ask prices. Generally speaking, when two parties wish to engage in a trade, the purchaser will announce a price he is willing to pay (the bid price) and seller will announce a price he is willing to accept (the ask price).

   a. Price mechanism
   b. 529 plan
   c. 7-Eleven
   d. 4-4-5 Calendar

22. The _____ for securities is the difference between the price quoted by a market maker for an immediate sale and an immediate purchase The size of the bid-offer spread in a given commodity is a measure of the liquidity of the market.

   The trader initiating the transaction is said to demand liquidity, and the other party to the transaction supplies liquidity.

   a. Trade-off
   b. Capital outflow
   c. Defined contribution plan
   d. Bid/offer spread

23. The value of speculative bonds is affected to a higher degree than investment grade bonds by the possibility of default. For example, in a recession interest rates may drop, and the drop in interest rates tends to increase the value of investment grade bonds; however, a recession tends to increase the possibility of default in speculative-grade bonds.

   The original speculative grade bonds were bonds that once had been investment grade at time of issue, but where the credit rating of the issuer had slipped and the possibility of default increased significantly. These bonds are called '_____'.

   a. Seed round
   b. Return on capital employed
   c. Fallen angels
   d. Sharpe ratio

24. In finance, a _____ (non-investment grade bond, speculative grade bond or junk bond) is a bond that is rated below investment grade at the time of purchase. These bonds have a higher risk of default or other adverse credit events, but typically pay higher yields than better quality bonds in order to make them attractive to investors.

Chapter 14. BOND ANALYSIS

a. Private equity
b. Sharpe ratio
c. Volatility
d. High yield bond

25. In business and accounting, _____s are everything of value that is owned by a person or company. The balance sheet of a firm records the monetary value of the _____s owned by the firm. The two major _____ classes are tangible _____s and intangible _____s.
   a. Accounts payable
   b. Income
   c. EBITDA
   d. Asset

26. In finance, _____ occurs when a debtor has not met its legal obligations according to the debt contract, e.g. it has not made a scheduled payment, or has violated a loan covenant (condition) of the debt contract. _____ may occur if the debtor is either unwilling or unable to pay their debt. This can occur with all debt obligations including bonds, mortgages, loans, and promissory notes.
   a. Default
   b. Credit crunch
   c. Vendor finance
   d. Debt validation

27. A _____ is a method of measuring a section of the stock market. Many indices are cited by news or financial services firms and are used to benchmark the performance of portfolios such as mutual funds.
   a. Stock market index
   b. Trading curb
   c. Stop order
   d. Program trading

28. In lending agreements, _____ is a borrower's pledge of specific property to a lender, to secure repayment of a loan. The _____ serves as protection for a lender against a borrower's risk of default - that is, a borrower failing to pay the principal and interest under the terms of a loan obligation. If a borrower does default on a loan (due to insolvency or other event), that borrower forfeits (gives up) the property pledged as _____ ollateral - and the lender then becomes the owner of the _____.
   a. Nominal value
   b. Future-oriented
   c. Refinancing risk
   d. Collateral

29. Established in 1973, The _____ was created to alleviate the rising volumes of paperwork and the lack of security that developed after rapid growth in the volume of transactions in the U.S. securities industry in the late 1960s.

Before _____ and NSCC were formed, brokers physically exchanged certificates, employing hundreds of messengers to carry certificates and checks. The mechanisms brokers used to transfer securities and keep records relied heavily on pen and paper.

   a. Wells Fargo ' Co.
   b. Federal Home Loan Mortgage Corporation
   c. Depository Trust Company
   d. Protect

30. A _____ is a corporation, especially a commercial bank, organized to perform the fiduciary functions of trusts and agencies. It is normally owned by one of three types of structures: an independent partnership, a bank, or a law firm, each of which specializes in being a trustee of various kinds of trusts and in managing estates.
   a. Trust Company
   b. Mutual fund
   c. Savings and loan association
   d. Person-to-person lending

31.

Chapter 14. BOND ANALYSIS

In finance, the _____ can be the expected rate of return above the risk-free interest rate. When measuring risk, a common sense approach is to compare the risk-free return on T-bills and the very risky return on other investments. The difference between these two returns can be interpreted as a measure of the excess return on the average risky asset. This excess return is known as the _____.

a. Risk premium
c. Risk aversion
b. Risk modeling
d. Risk adjusted return on capital

32. A _____ is a collective investment scheme that invests in bonds and other debt securities. _____s yield monthly dividends that include interest payments on the fund's underlying securities plus any capital appreciation in the prices of the portfolio's bonds. _____s tend to pay higher dividends than CDs and money market accounts, and they generally pay out dividends more frequently and regularly than individual bonds.

a. Gilts
c. Premium bond
b. Bond fund
d. Private activity bond

33. _____ refers to any type of investment that yields a regular (or fixed) return.

For example, if you lend money to a borrower and the borrower has to pay interest once a month, you have been issued a fixed-income security. When a company does this, it is often called a bond or corporate bank debt (although preferred stock is also sometimes considered to be _____).

a. Fixed Income
c. Bond market
b. 4-4-5 Calendar
d. 529 plan

34. _____ is a fee paid on borrowed assets. It is the price paid for the use of borrowed money, or, money earned by deposited funds. Assets that are sometimes lent with _____ include money, shares, consumer goods through hire purchase, major assets such as aircraft, and even entire factories in finance lease arrangements.

a. Interest
c. A Random Walk Down Wall Street
b. AAB
d. Insolvency

35. An _____ is the price a borrower pays for the use of money they do not own, and the return a lender receives for deferring the use of funds, by lending it to the borrower. _____s are normally expressed as a percentage rate over the period of one year.

_____s targets are also a vital tool of monetary policy and are used to control variables like investment, inflation, and unemployment.

a. ABN Amro
c. A Random Walk Down Wall Street
b. AAB
d. Interest rate

36. A _____ is a financial debt vehicle that was first created in June 1983 by investment banks Salomon Brothers and First Boston for Freddie Mac. (The First Boston team was led by Dexter Senft.) Legally, a _____ is a special purpose entity that is wholly separate from the institution(s) that create it.

Chapter 14. BOND ANALYSIS

a. 4-4-5 Calendar	b. Tranche
c. Yield curve spread	d. Collateralized mortgage obligation

37. A _____ is a fungible, negotiable instrument representing financial value. They are broadly categorized into debt securities (such as banknotes, bonds and debentures), and equity securities; e.g., common stocks. The company or other entity issuing the _____ is called the issuer.

a. Security	b. Tracking stock
c. Securities lending	d. Book entry

38. In finance, a _____ or accounting ratio is a ratio of two selected numerical values taken from an enterprise's financial statements. There are many standard ratios used to try to evaluate the overall financial condition of a corporation or other organization. They may be used by managers within a firm, by current and potential shareholders (owners) of a firm, and by a firm's creditors. Security analysts use these to compare the strengths and weaknesses in various companies.

a. Sustainable growth rate	b. Return on capital employed
c. Price/cash flow ratio	d. Financial ratio

Chapter 15. BOND PORTFOLIO MANAGEMENT

1. In finance, a _____ is a debt security, in which the authorized issuer owes the holders a debt and, depending on the terms of the _____, is obliged to pay interest (the coupon) and/or to repay the principal at a later date, termed maturity.

   Thus a _____ is a loan: the issuer is the borrower, the _____ holder is the lender, and the coupon is the interest. _____s provide the borrower with external funds to finance long-term investments, or, in the case of government _____s, to finance current expenditure.

   a. Convertible bond
   b. Catastrophe bonds
   c. Bond
   d. Puttable bond

2. The _____ is a financial market where participants buy and sell debt securities, usually in the form of bonds. As of 2006, the size of the international _____ is an estimated $45 trillion, of which the size of the outstanding U.S. _____ debt was $25.2 trillion.

   Nearly all of the $923 billion average daily trading volume in the U.S. _____ takes place between broker-dealers and large institutions in a decentralized, over-the-counter market.

   a. 4-4-5 Calendar
   b. 529 plan
   c. Fixed income
   d. Bond market

3. _____ is a fee paid on borrowed assets. It is the price paid for the use of borrowed money, or, money earned by deposited funds. Assets that are sometimes lent with _____ include money, shares, consumer goods through hire purchase, major assets such as aircraft, and even entire factories in finance lease arrangements.
   a. AAB
   b. A Random Walk Down Wall Street
   c. Insolvency
   d. Interest

4. An _____ is the price a borrower pays for the use of money they do not own, and the return a lender receives for deferring the use of funds, by lending it to the borrower. _____s are normally expressed as a percentage rate over the period of one year.

   _____s targets are also a vital tool of monetary policy and are used to control variables like investment, inflation, and unemployment.

   a. Interest rate
   b. AAB
   c. ABN Amro
   d. A Random Walk Down Wall Street

5. In finance, the _____ is the global financial market for short-term borrowing and lending. It provides short-term liquidity funding for the global financial system. The _____ is where short-term obligations such as Treasury bills, commercial paper and bankers' acceptances are bought and sold.
   a. Cramdown
   b. Debt-for-equity swap
   c. Consumer debt
   d. Money Market

6. _____ mature in one year or less. Like zero-coupon bonds, they do not pay interest prior to maturity; instead they are sold at a discount of the par value to create a positive yield to maturity. Many regard _____ as the least risky investment available to U.S. investors.

Chapter 15. BOND PORTFOLIO MANAGEMENT

a. Treasury securities
b. 4-4-5 Calendar
c. Treasury Inflation Protected Securities
d. Treasury bills

7. In statistics and signal processing, an _____ is a type of random process which is often used to model and predict various types of natural phenomena.

The notation AR(p) refers to the _____ of order p. The AR(p) model is defined as

$$X_t = c + \sum_{i=1}^{p} \varphi_i X_{t-i} + \varepsilon_t$$

where φ_i are the parameters of the model, c is a constant and ε_t is white noise.

a. ABN Amro
b. A Random Walk Down Wall Street
c. AAB
d. Autoregressive model

8. In economics, _____ is the total amount of money available in an economy at a particular point in time. There are several ways to define 'money', but each includes currency in circulation and demand deposits.

_____ data are recorded and published.

a. Money supply
b. 4-4-5 Calendar
c. 7-Eleven
d. 529 plan

9. A _____ is a person who makes investment decisions using money other people have placed under his or her control. In other words, it is a financial career involved in investment management. They work with a team of analysts and researchers, and are ultimately responsible for establishing an investment strategy, selecting appropriate investments and allocating each investment properly for a fund- or asset-management vehicle.

a. Portfolio manager
b. Purchasing manager
c. Financial analyst
d. Day trader

10. The coupon or _____ of a bond is the amount of interest paid per year expressed as a percentage of the face value of the bond.

For example if you hold $10,000 nominal of a bond described as a 4.5% loan stock, you will receive $450 in interest each year (probably in two installments of $225 each.)

Not all bonds have coupons.

a. Puttable bond
b. Zero-coupon bond
c. Coupon rate
d. Revenue bonds

Chapter 15. BOND PORTFOLIO MANAGEMENT

11. The _____ or redemption yield is the yield promised to the bondholder on the assumption that the bond or other fixed-interest security such as gilts will be held to maturity, that all coupon and principal payments will be made and coupon payments are reinvested at the bond's promised yield at the same rate as invested. It is a measure of the return of the bond. This technique in theory allows investors to calculate the fair value of different financial instruments.
    a. Yield to maturity
    b. Yield
    c. 4-4-5 Calendar
    d. Macaulay duration

12. In economics and finance, _____ is the practice of taking advantage of a price differential between two or more markets: striking a combination of matching deals that capitalize upon the imbalance, the profit being the difference between the market prices. When used by academics, an _____ is a transaction that involves no negative cash flow at any probabilistic or temporal state and a positive cash flow in at least one state; in simple terms, a risk-free profit.
    a. Efficient-market hypothesis
    b. Arbitrage
    c. Initial margin
    d. Issuer

13. _____, in finance, is a general theory of asset pricing, that has become influential in the pricing of stocks.

    _____ holds that the expected return of a financial asset can be modeled as a linear function of various macro-economic factors or theoretical market indices, where sensitivity to changes in each factor is represented by a factor-specific beta coefficient. The model-derived rate of return will then be used to price the asset correctly - the asset price should equal the expected end of period price discounted at the rate implied by model.

    a. ABN Amro
    b. Arbitrage pricing theory
    c. A Random Walk Down Wall Street
    d. AAB

14. In finance, the _____ of a financial asset measures the sensitivity of the asset's price to interest rate movements, expressed as a number of years. The reason for expressing this sensitivity in years is that the time that will elapse until a cash flow is received allows more interest to accumulate. Therefore the price of an asset with long term cashflows has more interest rate sensitivity than an asset with cashflows in the near future.
    a. Macaulay duration
    b. Yield to maturity
    c. 4-4-5 Calendar
    d. Duration

15. _____ is an international professional designation offered by the _____ Institute (formerly known as AIMR) to financial analysts who complete a series of three examinations. In order to become a '_____ Charterholder' candidates must pass all three six-hour exams, possess a bachelor's degree (or equivalent, as assessed by the _____ institute) and have 48 months of work experience in an investment decision-making position. _____ charterholders are also obligated to adhere to a strict Code of Ethics and Standards governing their professional conduct.
    a. 7-Eleven
    b. 4-4-5 Calendar
    c. 529 plan
    d. Chartered Financial Analyst

16. A _____, securities analyst, research analyst, equity analyst, or investment analyst is a person who performs financial analysis for external or internal clients as a core part of the job.

An analyst studies companies and other entities to arrive at the estimate of their financial value. It is normally done by analyzing financial reports, aided by follow-up interviews with company representatives and industry experts.

Chapter 15. BOND PORTFOLIO MANAGEMENT

    a. Purchasing manager   b. Portfolio manager
    c. Stockbroker   d. Financial Analyst

17. The _____ , largely the creation of Leo Melamed, is part of the Chicago Mercantile Exchange (CME), the largest futures exchange in the United States and the second largest in the world after Eurex, for the trading of futures contracts and options on futures. The _____ was started on May 16, 1972. Two of the more prevalent contracts traded are currency futures and interest rate futures.
    a. International Monetary Market   b. A Random Walk Down Wall Street
    c. AAB   d. ABN Amro

18. _____ is a combination of straight bond and embedded put option. The holder of the _____ has the right, but not the obligation, to demand early repayment of the principal. The put option is usually exercisable on specified dates.
    a. Callable bond   b. Brady bonds
    c. Convertible bond   d. Puttable bond

19. In lending agreements, _____ is a borrower's pledge of specific property to a lender, to secure repayment of a loan. The _____ serves as protection for a lender against a borrower's risk of default - that is, a borrower failing to pay the principal and interest under the terms of a loan obligation. If a borrower does default on a loan (due to insolvency or other event), that borrower forfeits (gives up) the property pledged as _____ *ollateral* - and the lender then becomes the owner of the _____ .
    a. Collateral   b. Nominal value
    c. Refinancing risk   d. Future-oriented

20. In finance, _____ occurs when a debtor has not met its legal obligations according to the debt contract, e.g. it has not made a scheduled payment, or has violated a loan covenant (condition) of the debt contract. _____ may occur if the debtor is either unwilling or unable to pay their debt. This can occur with all debt obligations including bonds, mortgages, loans, and promissory notes.
    a. Debt validation   b. Default
    c. Credit crunch   d. Vendor finance

21. An _____ is a contract written by a seller that conveys to the buyer the right -- but not the obligation -- to buy (in the case of a call _____) or to sell (in the case of a put _____) a particular asset, such as a piece of property such as, among others, a futures contract. In return for granting the _____, the seller collects a payment (the premium) from the buyer.

For example, buying a call _____ provides the right to buy a specified quantity of a security at a set strike price at some time on or before expiration, while buying a put _____ provides the right to sell.

    a. Amortization   b. AT'T Mobility LLC
    c. Option   d. Annuity

22. In finance, the term _____ describes the amount in cash that returns to the owners of a security. Normally it does not include the price variations, at the difference of the total return. _____ applies to various stated rates of return on stocks (common and preferred, and convertible), fixed income instruments (bonds, notes, bills, strips, zero coupon), and some other investment type insurance products (e.g. annuities.)

Chapter 15. BOND PORTFOLIO MANAGEMENT

a. 4-4-5 Calendar
c. Yield to maturity

b. Macaulay duration
d. Yield

23. In finance, the _____ is the relation between the interest rate (or cost of borrowing) and the time to maturity of the debt for a given borrower in a given currency. For example, the current U.S. dollar interest rates paid on U.S. Treasury securities for various maturities are closely watched by many traders, and are commonly plotted on a graph such as the one on the right which is informally called 'the _____.' More formal mathematical descriptions of this relation are often called the term structure of interest rates.

The yield of a debt instrument is the annualized percentage increase in the value of the investment.

a. 4-4-5 Calendar
c. 529 plan

b. 7-Eleven
d. Yield curve

24. _____ is the action of bringing a portfolio of investments that has deviated away from one's target asset allocation back into line. Under-weighted securities can be purchased with newly saved money; alternatively, over-weighted securities can be sold to purchase under-weighted securities.

The investments in a portfolio will perform according to the market.

a. Divestment
c. Security market line

b. Market timing
d. Rebalancing

25. A _____ is the counterpart to a deterministic process (or deterministic system) in probability theory. Instead of dealing with only one possible 'reality' of how the process might evolve under time (as is the case, for example, for solutions of an ordinary differential equation), in a stochastic or random process there is some indeterminacy in its future evolution described by probability distributions. This means that even if the initial condition (or starting point) is known, there are many possibilities the process might go to, but some paths are more probable and others less.

a. 529 plan
c. 7-Eleven

b. 4-4-5 Calendar
d. Stochastic process

26. _____ refers to a portfolio management strategy where the manager makes specific investments with the goal of outperforming an investment benchmark index. Investors or mutual funds that do not aspire to create a return in excess of a benchmark index will often invest in an index fund that replicates as closely as possible the investment weighting and returns of that index; this is called passive management. _____ is the opposite of passive management, because in passive management the manager does not seek to outperform the benchmark index.

a. ABN Amro
c. A Random Walk Down Wall Street

b. AAB
d. Active management

27. A _____ is a pool of assets forming an independent legal entity that are bought with the contributions to a pension plan for the exclusive purpose of financing pension plan benefits.

_____s are important shareholders of listed and private companies. They are especially important to the stock market where large institutional investors like the Ontario Teachers' Pension Plan dominate.

Chapter 15. BOND PORTFOLIO MANAGEMENT

a. Limited liability company
b. Pension fund
c. Leveraged buyout
d. Leverage

28. An _____ is an exchange of tangible assets for intangible assets or vice versa. Since it is a swap of assets, the procedure takes place on the active side of the balance sheet and has no impact on the latter in regards to volume. As an example, a company may sell equity and receive the value in cash thus increasing liquidity.
   a. Asset swap
   b. A Random Walk Down Wall Street
   c. ABN Amro
   d. AAB

29. In finance, a _____ is a derivative in which two counterparties agree to exchange one stream of cash flows against another stream. These streams are called the legs of the _____.

The cash flows are calculated over a notional principal amount, which is usually not exchanged between counterparties.

   a. Volatility swap
   b. Volatility arbitrage
   c. Local volatility
   d. Swap

30. _____ is a technique to adjust income payments by means of a price index, in order to maintain the purchasing power of the public after inflation.

Applying a cost-of-living escalation COLA clause to a stream of periodic payments protects the real value of those payments and effectively transfers the risk of inflation from the payee to the payor, who must pay more each year to reflect the increases in prices. Thus, inflation _____ is often applied to pension payments, rents and other situations which are not subject to regular re-pricing in the market.

   a. AAB
   b. Indexation
   c. ABN Amro
   d. A Random Walk Down Wall Street

31. The _____ is the tendency of the stock market to rise between December 31 and the end of the first week in January. There are many theories for why this happens, the main one being that it occurs because many investors choose to sell some of their stock right before the end of the year in order to claim a capital loss for tax purposes. Once the tax calendar rolls over to a new year on January 1st these same investors quickly reinvest their money in the market, causing stock prices to rise.
   a. Death spiral financing
   b. Sector rotation
   c. Revaluation
   d. January effect

32. _____ is a financial strategy in which a fund manager makes as few portfolio decisions as possible, in order to minimize transaction costs, including the incidence of capital gains tax. One popular method is to mimic the performance of an externally specified index--called 'index funds'. The ethos of an index fund is aptly summed up in the injunction to an index fund manager: 'Don't just do something, sit there!'

_____ is most common on the equity market, where index funds track a stock market index, but it is becoming more common in other investment types, including bonds, commodities and hedge funds.

Chapter 15. BOND PORTFOLIO MANAGEMENT

a. Trust company
c. Net asset value
b. Savings and loan association
d. Passive management

33. In statistics, _____ is a method of sampling from a population.

When sub-populations vary considerably, it is advantageous to sample each subpopulation (stratum) independently. Stratification is the process of grouping members of the population into relatively homogeneous subgroups before sampling.

a. Kurtosis
c. Mean
b. Stratified sampling
d. Correlation

34. In finance, _____ is a measure of how closely a portfolio follows the index to which it is benchmarked. It measures the standard deviation of the difference between the portfolio and index returns.

Many portfolios are managed to a benchmark, normally an index.

a. Transaction risk
c. Liquidity risk
b. Market risk
d. Tracking error

35. In business and accounting, _____s are everything of value that is owned by a person or company. The balance sheet of a firm records the monetary value of the _____s owned by the firm. The two major _____ classes are tangible _____s and intangible _____s.

a. Asset
c. Accounts payable
b. Income
d. EBITDA

36. _____ is a term used to refer to how an investor distributes his or her investments among various classes of investment vehicles (e.g., stocks and bonds.)

A large part of financial planning is finding an _____ that is appropriate for a given person in terms of their appetite for and ability to shoulder risk. This can depend on various factors; see investor profile.

a. Investing online
c. Investment performance
b. Asset allocation
d. Alternative investment

37. In business and finance, a _____ (also referred to as equity _____) of stock means a _____ of ownership in a corporation (company.) In the plural, stocks is often used as a synonym for _____s especially in the United States, but it is less commonly used that way outside of North America.

In the United Kingdom, South Africa, and Australia, stock can also refer to completely different financial instruments such as government bonds or, less commonly, to all kinds of marketable securities.

a. Margin
c. Procter ' Gamble
b. Bucket shop
d. Share

Chapter 16. COMMON STOCKS

1. _____ is a form of corporation equity ownership represented in the securities. It is dangerous in comparison to preferred shares and some other investment options, in that in the event of bankruptcy, _____ investors receive their funds after preferred stockholders, bondholders, creditors, etc. On the other hand, common shares on average perform better than preferred shares or bonds over time.

   a. Common stock
   b. Stop-limit order
   c. Stock market bubble
   d. Stock split

2. The institution most often referenced by the word '_____' is a public or publicly traded _____, the shares of which are traded on a public stock exchange (e.g., the New York Stock Exchange or Nasdaq in the United States) where shares of stock of _____s are bought and sold by and to the general public. Most of the largest businesses in the world are publicly traded _____s. However, the majority of _____s are said to be closely held, privately held or close _____s, meaning that no ready market exists for the trading of shares.

   a. Federal Home Loan Mortgage Corporation
   b. Corporation
   c. Depository Trust Company
   d. Protect

3. In business and finance, a _____ (also referred to as equity _____) of stock means a _____ of ownership in a corporation (company.) In the plural, stocks is often used as a synonym for _____s especially in the United States, but it is less commonly used that way outside of North America.

   In the United Kingdom, South Africa, and Australia, stock can also refer to completely different financial instruments such as government bonds or, less commonly, to all kinds of marketable securities.

   a. Bucket shop
   b. Procter ' Gamble
   c. Margin
   d. Share

4. A _____ is an event that may occur when a corporation's stockholders develop opposition to some aspect of the corporate governance, often focusing on directorial and management positions. Corporate activists may attempt to persuade shareholders to use their proxy votes (i.e. votes by one individual or institution as the authorized representative of another) to install new management for any of a variety of reasons.

   In a _____, incumbent directors and management have the odds stacked in their favor over those trying to force the corporate change.

   a. Procurement
   b. Forfaiting
   c. Trade finance
   d. Proxy fight

5. In corporate law, a _____ is a legal document that certifies ownership of a specific number of stock shares in a corporation. In large corporations, buying shares does not always lead to a _____

   Usually only shareholders with _____s can vote in a shareholders' general meeting.

   a. 529 plan
   b. 4-4-5 Calendar
   c. 7-Eleven
   d. Stock certificate

6. Companies that have publicly traded securities typically use _____ to keep track of the individuals and entities that own their stocks and bonds. Most _____ are banks or trust companies, but sometimes a company acts as its own transfer agent.

88   Chapter 16. COMMON STOCKS

_____ perform three main functions:

1. Issue and cancel certificates to reflect changes in ownership. For example, when a company declares a stock dividend or stock split, the transfer agent issues new shares. _____ keep records of who owns a company's stocks and bonds and how those stocks and bonds are held--whether by the owner in certificate form, by the company in book-entry form, or by the investor's brokerage firm in street name. They also keep records of how many shares or bonds each investor owns.
2. Act as an intermediary for the company. A transfer agent may also serve as the company's paying agent to pay out interest, cash and stock dividends, or other distributions to stock- and bondholders. In addition, _____ act as proxy agent (sending out proxy materials), exchange agent (exchanging a company's stock or bonds in a merger), tender agent (tendering shares in a tender offer), and mailing agent (mailing the company's quarterly, annual, and other reports.)
3. Handle lost, destroyed, or stolen certificates. _____ help shareholders and bondholders when a stock or bond certificate has been lost, destroyed, or stolen.

In many cases, you can find out which transfer agent a company uses by visiting the investor relations section of the company's website.

a. 529 plan
c. Transfer agents
b. 7-Eleven
d. 4-4-5 Calendar

7. _____ is a multiple-winner voting system intended to promote proportional representation while also being simple to understand.

_____ is used frequently in corporate governance, where it is mandated by many U.S. states, and it was used to elect the Illinois House of Representatives from 1870 until its repeal in 1980. It was used in England in the late 19th century to elect school boards.

a. 529 plan
c. Cumulative voting
b. 4-4-5 Calendar
d. 7-Eleven

8. _____ is money paid by a company (or allied company or individual) to acquire its own shares of stock from a shareholder who is threatening to take control of, or unwanted influence of, the company.

The term is a neologism combining the terms greenback and blackmail, invented by journalists and commentators who saw the practices of corporate raiders as a form of blackmail. The target company is financially held hostage, and is legally forced to pay the _____er to go away.

a. Stock swap
c. 4-4-5 Calendar
b. 529 plan
d. Greenmail

9. The _____ is a defensive option to stave off a hostile takeover in which a company that is threatened with a hostile takeover acquires its would-be buyer.

Chapter 16. COMMON STOCKS

The most quoted example in U.S. corporate history is the attempted hostile takeover of Martin Marietta by Bendix Corporation in 1982. In response, Martin Marietta started buying Bendix stock with the aim of assuming control over the company.

a. Pac-Man defense
b. Procurement
c. Proxy fight
d. Golden parachute

10. In business, a _____ is the purchase of one company (the target) by another (the acquirer or bidder). In the UK the term refers to the acquisition of a public company whose shares are listed on a stock exchange, in contrast to the acquisition of a private company.

Before a bidder makes an offer for another company, it usually first informs that company's board of directors.

a. Stock swap
b. Takeover
c. 529 plan
d. 4-4-5 Calendar

11. _____ is a corporate finance term denoting a type of takeover bid. The _____ is a public, open offer or invitation (usually announced in a newspaper advertisement) by a prospective acquirer to all stockholders of a publicly traded corporation (the target corporation) to tender their stock for sale at a specified price during a specified time, subject to the tendering of a minimum and maximum number of shares. In a _____, the bidder contacts shareholders directly; the directors of the company may or may not have endorsed the _____ proposal.

a. Cash is king
b. Follow-on offering
c. Tender offer
d. Shareholder value

12. In accounting, _____ or *Carrying value* is the value of an asset according to its balance sheet account balance. For assets, the value is based on the original cost of the asset less any depreciation, amortization or impairment costs made against the asset. A company's _____ is its total assets minus intangible assets and liabilities.

a. Book value
b. Pro forma
c. Retained earnings
d. Current liabilities

13. _____, in finance and accounting, means stated value or face value. From this comes the expressions at par (at the _____), over par (over _____) and under par (under _____.)

The term '_____' has several meanings depending on context and geography.

a. FIDC
b. Par value
c. Sinking fund
d. Global Squeeze

14. _____ is a system of tracking ownership of securities where no certificate is given to investors. In the case of _____ only issues, while investors do not receive certificates, a custodian holds one or more global certificates. Dematerialized securities, in contrast are ones in which no certificates exist (instead, the security issuer or its agent keeps records, usually electronically, of who holds outstanding securities.)

a. Securities lending
b. Tracking stock
c. Book entry
d. Marketable

Chapter 16. COMMON STOCKS

15. _____ is the set of processes, customs, policies, laws and institutions affecting the way a corporation is directed, administered or controlled. _____ also includes the relationships among the many stakeholders involved and the goals for which the corporation is governed. The principal stakeholders are the shareholders, management and the board of directors.
   a. Due diligence
   b. Foreign Corrupt Practices Act
   c. Corporate governance
   d. Patent

16. In economics, _____ is a rise in the general level of prices of goods and services in an economy over a period of time. The term '_____' once referred to increases in the money supply (monetary _____); however, economic debates about the relationship between money supply and price levels have led to its primary use today in describing price _____. _____ can also be described as a decline in the real value of money--a loss of purchasing power in the medium of exchange which is also the monetary unit of account.
   a. ABN Amro
   b. AAB
   c. A Random Walk Down Wall Street
   d. Inflation

17. _____ are organizations which pool large sums of money and invest those sums in companies. They include banks, insurance companies, retirement or pension funds, hedge funds and mutual funds. Their role in the economy is to act as highly specialized investors on behalf of others.
   a. A Random Walk Down Wall Street
   b. AAB
   c. ABN Amro
   d. Institutional Investors

18. A _____ or reacquired stock is stock which is bought back by the issuing company, reducing the amount of outstanding stock on the open market ('open market' including insiders' holdings.)

Stock repurchases are often used as a tax-efficient method to put cash into shareholders' hands, rather than pay dividends. Sometimes, companies do this when they feel that their stock is undervalued on the open market.

   a. Trial balance
   b. Current asset
   c. Generally Accepted Accounting Principles
   d. Treasury stock

19. In economics and finance, _____ is the practice of taking advantage of a price differential between two or more markets: striking a combination of matching deals that capitalize upon the imbalance, the profit being the difference between the market prices. When used by academics, an _____ is a transaction that involves no negative cash flow at any probabilistic or temporal state and a positive cash flow in at least one state; in simple terms, a risk-free profit.
   a. Efficient-market hypothesis
   b. Issuer
   c. Initial margin
   d. Arbitrage

20. The key date to remember for dividend paying stocks is the _____. The _____ is different from the record date. The _____ is typically two trading days before the record date.

In order to receive the upcoming dividend payment payout, you must already own or you must purchase the stock prior to the _____. It is important to note that in most countries, when you buy or sell any stock, there is a three trading-day settlement period on your order.

Chapter 16. COMMON STOCKS

a. Asian Financial Crisis
b. Ex-dividend date
c. Insolvency
d. Index number

21. _____, refers to consumption opportunity gained by an entity within a specified time frame, which is generally expressed in monetary terms. However, for households and individuals, '_____ is the sum of all the wages, salaries, profits, interests payments, rents and other forms of earnings received... in a given period of time.' For firms, _____ generally refers to net-profit: what remains of revenue after expenses have been subtracted.

a. Annual report
b. Income
c. OIBDA
d. Accrual

22. An _____ is a tax levied on the financial income of people, corporations, or other legal entities. Various _____ systems exist, with varying degrees of tax incidence. Income taxation can be progressive, proportional, or regressive.

a. ABN Amro
b. AAB
c. A Random Walk Down Wall Street
d. Income Tax

23. _____ refers to stock of a company that is not fully transferable until certain conditions have been met. Upon satisfaction of those conditions, the stock becomes transferable by the person holding the award.

Another type of _____ is a form of compensation granted by a company. Typically, the conditions that allow the shares to be transferred are a period of time, when they vest.

a. Shareholder value
b. Restricted stock
c. Market for corporate control
d. Cash flow

24. In the United States, a _____ is an offering of securities that are not registered with the Securities and Exchange Commission (SEC.) Such offerings exploit an exemption offered by the Securities Act of 1933 that comes with several restrictions, including a prohibition against general solicitation. This exemption allows companies to avoid quarterly reporting requirements and many of the legal liabilities associated with the Sarbanes-Oxley Act.

a. Private placement
b. 529 plan
c. 4-4-5 Calendar
d. 7-Eleven

25. A _____ is a payment made by a corporation to its shareholder members. When a corporation earns a profit or surplus, that money can be put to two uses: it can either be re-invested in the business (called retained earnings), or it can be paid to the shareholders as a _____. Many corporations retain a portion of their earnings and pay the remainder as a _____.

a. Dividend yield
b. Dividend puzzle
c. Special dividend
d. Dividend

26. On a stock exchange, a _____ is the opposite of a stock split, i.e. a stock merge - a reduction in the number of shares and an accompanying increase in the share price. The ratio is also reversed: 1-for-2, 1-for-3 and so on.

There is a stigma attached to doing this so it is not initiated without very good reason.

Chapter 16. COMMON STOCKS

a. Conglomerate merger
c. Correlation trading
b. Trade date
d. Reverse stock split

27. _____ are those dividends paid out in form of additional stock shares of the issuing corporation or other corporation They are usually issued in proportion to shares owned (for example for every 100 shares of stock owned, 5% stock dividend will yield 5 extra shares). If this payment involves the issue of new shares, this is very similar to a stock split in that it increases the total number of shares while lowering the price of each share and does not change the market capitalization or the total value of the shares held
a. The Hong Kong Securities Institute
c. Stock or scrip dividends
b. Time-based currency
d. Database auditing

28. A _____ or stock divide increases or decreases the number of shares in a public company. The price is adjusted such that the before and after market capitalization of the company remains the same and dilution does not occur. Options and warrants are included.
a. Stop order
c. Stock split
b. Contract for difference
d. Stop price

29. A _____ is a right to acquire certain property in preference to any other person. It usually refers to property newly coming into existence. A right to acquire existing property in preference to any other person is usually referred to as a right of first refusal.

In practice, the most common form of _____ is the right of existing shareholders to acquire newly issued shares issued by a company in a rights issue, a usually but not always public offering.

a. Court of Audit of Belgium
c. Down payment
b. Fraud deterrence
d. Pre-emption right

30. The _____ on a company stock is the company's annual dividend payments divided by its market cap, or the dividend per share divided by the price per share. It is often expressed as a percentage.

Dividend payments on preferred shares are stipulated by the prospectus.

a. Dividend reinvestment plan
c. Dividend yield
b. Special dividend
d. Dividend imputation

31. The _____ is an American stock exchange. It is the largest electronic screen-based equity securities trading market in the United States. With approximately 3,200 companies, it has more trading volume per day than any other stock exchange in the world.
a. 4-4-5 Calendar
c. 7-Eleven
b. Nasdaq
d. 529 plan

32. In the United States, the Financial Industry Regulatory Authority (FINRA) is a self-regulatory organization (SRO) under the Securities Exchange Act of 1934, successor to the _____, Inc.

Chapter 16. COMMON STOCKS

FINRA is responsible for regulatory oversight of all securities firms that do business with the public; professional training, testing and licensing of registered persons; arbitration and mediation; market regulation by contract for The NASDAQ Stock Market, Inc., the American Stock Exchange LLC, and the International Securities Exchange, LLC; and industry utilities, such as Trade Reporting Facilities and other over-the-counter operations.

- a. 7-Eleven
- b. 4-4-5 Calendar
- c. 529 plan
- d. National Association of Securities Dealers

33. A _____ is a fungible, negotiable instrument representing financial value. They are broadly categorized into debt securities (such as banknotes, bonds and debentures), and equity securities; e.g., common stocks. The company or other entity issuing the _____ is called the issuer.
- a. Security
- b. Securities lending
- c. Book entry
- d. Tracking stock

34. In finance, the term _____ describes the amount in cash that returns to the owners of a security. Normally it does not include the price variations, at the difference of the total return. _____ applies to various stated rates of return on stocks (common and preferred, and convertible), fixed income instruments (bonds, notes, bills, strips, zero coupon), and some other investment type insurance products (e.g. annuities.)
- a. Yield to maturity
- b. 4-4-5 Calendar
- c. Yield
- d. Macaulay duration

35. In finance, a _____ is a debt security, in which the authorized issuer owes the holders a debt and, depending on the terms of the _____, is obliged to pay interest (the coupon) and/or to repay the principal at a later date, termed maturity.

Thus a _____ is a loan: the issuer is the borrower, the _____ holder is the lender, and the coupon is the interest. _____s provide the borrower with external funds to finance long-term investments, or, in the case of government _____s, to finance current expenditure.

- a. Bond
- b. Puttable bond
- c. Convertible bond
- d. Catastrophe bonds

36. A _____, securities exchange or (in Europe) bourse is a corporation or mutual organization which provides 'trading' facilities for stock brokers and traders, to trade stocks and other securities. _____s also provide facilities for the issue and redemption of securities as well as other financial instruments and capital events including the payment of income and dividends. The securities traded on a _____ include: shares issued by companies, unit trusts and other pooled investment products and bonds.
- a. 7-Eleven
- b. 4-4-5 Calendar
- c. 529 plan
- d. Stock exchange

37. The _____ is a stock exchange based in New York City, New York. It is the largest stock exchange in the world by dollar value of its listed companies securities. As of October 2008, the combined capitalization of all domestic _____ listed companies was $10.1 trillion.

Chapter 16. COMMON STOCKS

a. New York Stock Exchange
b. 7-Eleven
c. 4-4-5 Calendar
d. 529 plan

38. An _____ is a contract written by a seller that conveys to the buyer the right -- but not the obligation -- to buy (in the case of a call _____) or to sell (in the case of a put _____) a particular asset, such as a piece of property such as, among others, a futures contract. In return for granting the _____, the seller collects a payment (the premium) from the buyer.

For example, buying a call _____ provides the right to buy a specified quantity of a security at a set strike price at some time on or before expiration, while buying a put _____ provides the right to sell.

a. Option
b. AT'T Mobility LLC
c. Amortization
d. Annuity

39. The method of least squares or _____ is used to approximately solve overdetermined systems. Least squares is often applied in statistical contexts, particularly regression analysis.

Least squares can be interpreted as a method of fitting data.

a. ABN Amro
b. AAB
c. A Random Walk Down Wall Street
d. Ordinary least squares

40. In probability and statistics, the _____ of a collection of numbers is a measure of the dispersion of the numbers from their expected (mean) value. It can apply to a probability distribution, a random variable, a population or a data set. The _____ is usually denoted with the letter σ (lowercase sigma.)

a. Kurtosis
b. Sample size
c. Mean
d. Standard deviation

41. In statistics, _____ is used for two things;

- to construct a simple formula that will predict a value or values for a variable given the value of another variable.
- to test whether and how a given variable is related to another variable or variables.

_____ is a form of regression analysis in which the relationship between one or more independent variables and another variable, called the dependent variable, is modelled by a least squares function, called a _____ equation. This function is a linear combination of one or more model parameters, called regression coefficients. A _____ equation with one independent variable represents a straight line when the predicted value (i.e. the dependant variable from the regression equation) is plotted against the independent variable: this is called a simple _____. However, note that 'linear' does not refer to this straight line, but rather to the way in which the regression coefficients occur in the regression equation.

a. Foreign Language and Area Studies
b. Wall Street Crash of 1929
c. Stock trader
d. Linear regression

Chapter 16. COMMON STOCKS

42. A _____ is a linear regression in which there is only one covariate (predictor variable.)

_____ is used to evaluate the linear relationship between two variables. One example could be the relationship between muscle strength and lean body mass.

   a. 7-Eleven
   b. 4-4-5 Calendar
   c. 529 plan
   d. Simple linear regression

43. _____ is a risk-adjusted measure of the so-called active return on an investment. It is the return in excess of the compensation for the risk borne, and thus commonly used to assess active managers' performances. Often, the return of a benchmark is subtracted in order to consider relative performance, which yields Jensen's _____.
   a. Amortization
   b. Annuity
   c. Option
   d. Alpha

44. The _____, in terms of finance and investing, describes how the expected return of a stock or portfolio is correlated to the return of the financial market as a whole.

An asset with a beta of 0 means that its price is not at all correlated with the market; that asset is independent. A positive beta means that the asset generally follows the market.

   a. LIBOR market model
   b. Perpetuity
   c. Current yield
   d. Beta coefficient

45. In statistics, the _____, R^2 is used in the context of statistical models whose main purpose is the prediction of future outcomes on the basis of other related information. It is the proportion of variability in a data set that is accounted for by the statistical model. It provides a measure of how well future outcomes are likely to be predicted by the model.
   a. 529 plan
   b. Coefficient of determination
   c. 7-Eleven
   d. 4-4-5 Calendar

46. In statistics, _____ or explained randomness measures the proportion to which a mathematical model accounts for the variation (= apparent randomness) of a given data set. Often, variation is quantified as variance; then, the more specific term explained variance can be used.

The complementary part of the total variation/randomness/variance is called unexplained or residual.

   a. ABN Amro
   b. AAB
   c. Explained variation
   d. A Random Walk Down Wall Street

47. A _____ is a type of auction where the auctioneer begins with a high asking price which is lowered until some participant is willing to accept the auctioneer's price, or a predetermined reserve price (the seller's minimum acceptable price) is reached. The winning participant pays the last announced price. This is also known as a 'clock auction' or an open-outcry descending-price auction.
   a. 4-4-5 Calendar
   b. 7-Eleven
   c. 529 plan
   d. Dutch auction

Chapter 16. COMMON STOCKS

48. In finance, _____ are stocks that appreciate in value and yield a high return on equity (ROE.) Analysts compute ROE by taking the company's net income and dividing it by the company's equity. To be classified as a growth stock, analysts expect to see at least 15 percent return on equity.
   a. 4-4-5 Calendar
   b. Security Analysis
   c. Stock valuation
   d. Growth stocks

49. _____ is typically a higher ranking stock than voting shares, and its terms are negotiated between the corporation and the investor.

   _____ usually carry no voting rights, but may carry superior priority over common stock in the payment of dividends and upon liquidation. _____ may carry a dividend that is paid out prior to any dividends to common stock holders.

   a. Follow-on offering
   b. Trade-off theory
   c. Second lien loan
   d. Preferred stock

50. The _____ is that part of the capital markets that deals with the issuance of new securities. Companies, governments or public sector institutions can obtain funding through the sale of a new stock or bond issue. This is typically done through a syndicate of securities dealers.
   a. Volatility clustering
   b. Sector rotation
   c. Peer group analysis
   d. Primary market

51. A _____ or bank is a financial institution whose primary activity is to act as a payment agent for customers and to borrow and lend money.

   The first modern bank was founded in Italy in Genoa in 1406, its name was Banco di San Giorgio (Bank of St. George.)

   Many other financial activities were added over time.

   a. Banker
   b. 4-4-5 Calendar
   c. Black Sea Trade and Development Bank
   d. Bought deal

52. _____ is the acquisition of goods and/or services at the best possible total cost of ownership, in the right quantity and quality, at the right time, in the right place and from the right source for the direct benefit or use of corporations or individuals, generally via a contract. Simple _____ may involve nothing more than repeat purchasing. Complex _____ could involve finding long term partners - or even 'co-destiny' suppliers that might fundamentally commit one organization to another.
   a. Pac-Man defense
   b. Procurement
   c. Market capitalization
   d. Synthetic CDO

53. _____ refers to any type of investment that yields a regular (or fixed) return.

For example, if you lend money to a borrower and the borrower has to pay interest once a month, you have been issued a fixed-income security. When a company does this, it is often called a bond or corporate bank debt (although preferred stock is also sometimes considered to be _____).

Chapter 16. COMMON STOCKS

a. 529 plan
b. Fixed Income
c. Bond market
d. 4-4-5 Calendar

54. _____, is when a company issues common stock or shares to the public for the first time. They are often issued by smaller, younger companies seeking capital to expand, but can also be done by large privately-owned companies looking to become publicly traded.

In an _____ the issuer may obtain the assistance of an underwriting firm, which helps it determine what type of security to issue (common or preferred), best offering price and time to bring it to market.

a. Interest
b. Insolvency
c. Asian Financial Crisis
d. Initial public offering

55. _____ is an arrangement with the U.S. Securities and Exchange Commission that allows a single registration document to be filed that permits the issuance of multiple securities.

_____ is a registration of a new issue which can be prepared up to two years in advance, so that the issue can be offered quickly as soon as funds are needed or market conditions are favorable.

For example, current market conditions in the housing market are not favorable for a specific firm to issue a public offering.

a. Bought deal
b. 4-4-5 Calendar
c. Black Sea Trade and Development Bank
d. Shelf registration

56. A _____ is an international bond that is denominated in a currency not native to the country where it is issued. It can be categorised according to the currency in which it is issued. London is one of the centers of the _____ market, but _____s may be traded throughout the world - for example in Singapore or Tokyo.

a. Interest rate option
b. Economic entity
c. Education production function
d. Eurobond

57. In finance, a _____ (non-investment grade bond, speculative grade bond or junk bond) is a bond that is rated below investment grade at the time of purchase. These bonds have a higher risk of default or other adverse credit events, but typically pay higher yields than better quality bonds in order to make them attractive to investors.

a. Volatility
b. Private equity
c. Sharpe ratio
d. High yield bond

58. The U.S. _____ is an independent agency of the United States government which holds primary responsibility for enforcing the federal securities laws and regulating the securities industry, the nation's stock and options exchanges, and other electronic securities markets. The SEC was created by section 4 of the SEC of 1934 (now codified as 15 U.S.C. Â§ 78d and commonly referred to as the 1934 Act.)

a. 7-Eleven
b. 529 plan
c. 4-4-5 Calendar
d. Securities and Exchange Commission

59. A _____ is a private or public market for the trading of company stock and derivatives of company stock at an agreed price; these are securities listed on a stock exchange as well as those only traded privately.

Chapter 16. COMMON STOCKS

The size of the world _____ is estimated at about $36.6 trillion US at the beginning of October 2008 . The world derivatives market has been estimated at about $480 trillion face or nominal value, 12 times the size of the entire world economy.

a. Anton Gelonkin
c. Andrew Tobias
b. Adolph Coors
d. Stock market

60. In economic models, the _____ time frame assumes no fixed factors of production. Firms can enter or leave the marketplace, and the cost (and availability) of land, labor, raw materials, and capital goods can be assumed to vary. In contrast, in the short-run time frame, certain factors are assumed to be fixed, because there is not sufficient time for them to change.

a. 4-4-5 Calendar
c. Long-run
b. 529 plan
d. Short-run

61. The _____ is the tendency of the stock market to rise between December 31 and the end of the first week in January. There are many theories for why this happens, the main one being that it occurs because many investors choose to sell some of their stock right before the end of the year in order to claim a capital loss for tax purposes. Once the tax calendar rolls over to a new year on January 1st these same investors quickly reinvest their money in the market, causing stock prices to rise.

a. Revaluation
c. Death spiral financing
b. January effect
d. Sector rotation

62. The _____ is a financial market where participants buy and sell debt securities, usually in the form of bonds. As of 2006, the size of the international _____ is an estimated $45 trillion, of which the size of the outstanding U.S. _____ debt was $25.2 trillion.

Nearly all of the $923 billion average daily trading volume in the U.S. _____ takes place between broker-dealers and large institutions in a decentralized, over-the-counter market.

a. 4-4-5 Calendar
c. 529 plan
b. Bond market
d. Fixed income

63. _____ means regulating, adapting or settling in a variety of contexts:

In commercial law, _____ means the settlement of a loss incurred on insured goods. The calculation of the amounts of compensation to be paid by or to the several interests is a complicated matter. It involves much detail and arithmetic, and requires a full and accurate knowledge of the principles of the subject.

a. Asset recovery
c. Equity method
b. Adjustment
d. Intelligent investor

64. In finance, _____ (or gearing) is borrowing money to supplement existing funds for investment in such a way that the potential positive or negative outcome is magnified and/or enhanced. It generally refers to using borrowed funds, or debt, so as to attempt to increase the returns to equity. Deleveraging is the action of reducing borrowings.

Chapter 16. COMMON STOCKS

a. Pension fund
c. Financial endowment
b. Limited partnership
d. Leverage

65. In financial and business accounting, _____ is a measure of a firm's profitability that excludes interest and income tax expenses.

EBIT = Operating Revenue - Operating Expenses (OPEX) + Non-operating Income

Operating Income = Operating Revenue - Operating Expenses

Operating income is the difference between operating revenues and operating expenses, but it is also sometimes used as a synonym for EBIT and operating profit. This is true if the firm has no non-operating income.

a. ABN Amro
c. AAB
b. A Random Walk Down Wall Street
d. Earnings before interest and taxes

66. _____ is a fee paid on borrowed assets. It is the price paid for the use of borrowed money, or, money earned by deposited funds. Assets that are sometimes lent with _____ include money, shares, consumer goods through hire purchase, major assets such as aircraft, and even entire factories in finance lease arrangements.
a. AAB
c. Interest
b. Insolvency
d. A Random Walk Down Wall Street

Chapter 17. THE VALUATION OF COMMON STOCKS

1. _____ is a form of corporation equity ownership represented in the securities. It is dangerous in comparison to preferred shares and some other investment options, in that in the event of bankruptcy, _____ investors receive their funds after preferred stockholders, bondholders, creditors, etc. On the other hand, common shares on average perform better than preferred shares or bonds over time.
    a. Stock market bubble
    b. Common stock
    c. Stock split
    d. Stop-limit order

2. A '_____' is a 'Charge' that is paid to obtain the right to delay a payment. Essentially, the payer purchases the right to make a given payment in the future instead of in the Present. The '_____', or 'Charge' that must be paid to delay the payment, is simply the difference between what the payment amount would be if it were paid in the present and what the payment amount would be paid if it were paid in the future.
    a. Value at risk
    b. Risk modeling
    c. Risk aversion
    d. Discount

3. The _____ is an interest rate a central bank charges depository institutions that borrow reserves from it.

The term _____ has two meanings:

- the same as interest rate; the term 'discount' does not refer to the meaning of the word, but to the purpose of using the quantity, such as computations of present value, e.g. net present value / discounted cash flow

- the annual effective _____, which is the annual interest divided by the capital including that interest; this rate is lower than the interest rate; it corresponds to using the value after a year as the nominal value, and seeing the initial value as the nominal value minus a discount; it is used for Treasury Bills and similar financial instruments

The annual effective _____ is the annual interest divided by the capital including that interest, which is the interest rate divided by 100% plus the interest rate. It is the annual discount factor to be applied to the future cash flow, to find the discount, subtracted from a future value to find the value one year earlier.

For example, suppose there is a government bond that sells for $95 and pays $100 in a year's time.

    a. Stochastic volatility
    b. Black-Scholes
    c. Fisher equation
    d. Discount rate

4. _____, refers to consumption opportunity gained by an entity within a specified time frame, which is generally expressed in monetary terms. However, for households and individuals, '_____ is the sum of all the wages, salaries, profits, interests payments, rents and other forms of earnings received... in a given period of time.' For firms, _____ generally refers to net-profit: what remains of revenue after expenses have been subtracted.
    a. OIBDA
    b. Accrual
    c. Annual report
    d. Income

5. A _____, securities exchange or (in Europe) bourse is a corporation or mutual organization which provides 'trading' facilities for stock brokers and traders, to trade stocks and other securities. _____s also provide facilities for the issue and redemption of securities as well as other financial instruments and capital events including the payment of income and dividends. The securities traded on a _____ include: shares issued by companies, unit trusts and other pooled investment products and bonds.

Chapter 17. THE VALUATION OF COMMON STOCKS

a. 4-4-5 Calendar
b. 529 plan
c. 7-Eleven
d. Stock exchange

6. _____ is an estimate of the fair value of corporations and their stocks, by using fundamental economic criteria. This theoretical valuation has to be perfected with market criteria, as the final purpose is to determine potential market prices.
   a. Stock valuation
   b. Growth stocks
   c. 4-4-5 Calendar
   d. Security Analysis

7. In finance, _____ is the process of estimating the potential market value of a financial asset or liability. they can be done on assets (for example, investments in marketable securities such as stocks, options, business enterprises, or intangible assets such as patents and trademarks) or on liabilities (e.g., Bonds issued by a company.) _____s are required in many contexts including investment analysis, capital budgeting, merger and acquisition transactions, financial reporting, taxable events to determine the proper tax liability, and in litigation.
   a. Share
   b. Margin
   c. Valuation
   d. Procter ' Gamble

8. The _____ is a capital budgeting metric used by firms to decide whether they should make investments. It is an indicator of the efficiency or quality of an investment, as opposed to net present value (NPV), which indicates value or magnitude.

The IRR is the annualized effective compounded return rate which can be earned on the invested capital, i.e., the yield on the investment.

   a. AAB
   b. ABN Amro
   c. A Random Walk Down Wall Street
   d. Internal rate of return

9. _____ is equal to the income that a firm has after subtracting costs and expenses from the total revenue. _____ can be distributed among holders of common stock as a dividend or held by the firm as retained earnings. _____ is an accounting term; in some countries (such as the UK) profit is the usual term.
   a. Write-off
   b. Historical cost
   c. Furniture, Fixtures and Equipment
   d. Net income

10. _____ or net present worth (NPW) is defined as the total present value (PV) of a time series of cash flows. It is a standard method for using the time value of money to appraise long-term projects. Used for capital budgeting, and widely throughout economics, it measures the excess or shortfall of cash flows, in present value terms, once financing charges are met.
    a. Present value of costs
    b. Tax shield
    c. Negative gearing
    d. Net present value

11. _____ is the value on a given date of a future payment or series of future payments, discounted to reflect the time value of money and other factors such as investment risk. _____ calculations are widely used in business and economics to provide a means to compare cash flows at different times on a meaningful 'like to like' basis.

The most commonly applied model of the time value of money is compound interest.

Chapter 17. THE VALUATION OF COMMON STOCKS

a. Present value of benefits
b. Negative gearing
c. Net present value
d. Present value

12. In finance, _____, also known as return on investment is the ratio of money gained or lost on an investment relative to the amount of money invested. The amount of money gained or lost may be referred to as interest, profit/loss, gain/loss, or net income/loss. The money invested may be referred to as the asset, capital, principal, or the cost basis of the investment.
a. Composiition of Creditors
b. Doctrine of the Proper Law
c. Stock or scrip dividends
d. Rate of return

13. A _____ is a payment made by a corporation to its shareholder members. When a corporation earns a profit or surplus, that money can be put to two uses: it can either be re-invested in the business (called retained earnings), or it can be paid to the shareholders as a _____. Many corporations retain a portion of their earnings and pay the remainder as a _____.
a. Special dividend
b. Dividend puzzle
c. Dividend yield
d. Dividend

14. In business and finance, a _____ (also referred to as equity _____) of stock means a _____ of ownership in a corporation (company.) In the plural, stocks is often used as a synonym for _____s especially in the United States, but it is less commonly used that way outside of North America.

In the United Kingdom, South Africa, and Australia, stock can also refer to completely different financial instruments such as government bonds or, less commonly, to all kinds of marketable securities.

a. Share
b. Margin
c. Bucket shop
d. Procter ' Gamble

15. A _____ rocket is a rocket that uses two or more stages, each of which contains its own engines and propellant. A tandem or serial stage is mounted on top of another stage; a parallel stage is attached alongside another stage. The result is effectively two or more rockets stacked on top of or attached next to each other.
a. 4-4-5 Calendar
b. 529 plan
c. 7-Eleven
d. Multistage

16. _____ is the fraction of net income a firm pays to its stockholders in dividends:

The part of the earnings not paid to investors is left for investment to provide for future earnings growth. Investors seeking high current income and limited capital growth prefer companies with high _____. However investors seeking capital growth may prefer lower payout ratio because capital gains are taxed at a lower rate.

a. Dividend yield
b. Dividend payout ratio
c. Dividend imputation
d. Dividend puzzle

Chapter 17. THE VALUATION OF COMMON STOCKS

17. In investments, _____ refers to the annual rate of growth of earnings. When the dividend payout ratio is the same, the dividend growth rate is equal to the _____ rate.

_____ rate is a key value that is needed when the DCF model, or the Gordon's model is used for stock valuation.

   a. Annuity
   c. Alternative asset
   b. Alternative display facility
   d. Earnings growth

18. A _____ is a fungible, negotiable instrument representing financial value. They are broadly categorized into debt securities (such as banknotes, bonds and debentures), and equity securities; e.g., common stocks. The company or other entity issuing the _____ is called the issuer.
   a. Security
   c. Tracking stock
   b. Securities lending
   d. Book entry

19. In Modern Portfolio Theory, the _____ is the graphical representation of the Capital Asset Pricing Model. It displays the expected rate of return for an overall market as a function of systematic (non-diversifiable) risk (beta.)

The Y-Intercept (beta=0) of the _____ is equal to the risk-free interest rate.

   a. Rebalancing
   c. Divestment
   b. Certificate in Investment Performance Measurement
   d. Security market line

20. _____ is a risk-adjusted measure of the so-called active return on an investment. It is the return in excess of the compensation for the risk borne, and thus commonly used to assess active managers' performances. Often, the return of a benchmark is subtracted in order to consider relative performance, which yields Jensen's _____.
   a. Annuity
   c. Option
   b. Amortization
   d. Alpha

21. The _____ is the weighted-average most likely outcome in gambling, probability theory, economics or finance.

In gambling and probability theory, there is usually a discrete set of possible outcomes. In this case, _____ is a measure of the relative balance of win or loss weighted by their chances of occurring.

   a. Expected return
   c. A Random Walk Down Wall Street
   b. ABN Amro
   d. AAB

22. A _____ is a private or public market for the trading of company stock and derivatives of company stock at an agreed price; these are securities listed on a stock exchange as well as those only traded privately.

The size of the world _____ is estimated at about $36.6 trillion US at the beginning of October 2008 . The world derivatives market has been estimated at about $480 trillion face or nominal value, 12 times the size of the entire world economy.

a. Adolph Coors
b. Anton Gelonkin
c. Andrew Tobias
d. Stock market

Chapter 18. EARNINGS

1. A _____ is a payment made by a corporation to its shareholder members. When a corporation earns a profit or surplus, that money can be put to two uses: it can either be re-invested in the business (called retained earnings), or it can be paid to the shareholders as a _____. Many corporations retain a portion of their earnings and pay the remainder as a _____.

   a. Special dividend
   b. Dividend puzzle
   c. Dividend yield
   d. Dividend

2. The _____, in Corporate finance, is a decision made by the directors of a company. It relates to the amount and timing of any cash payments made to the company's stockholders. The decision is an important one for the firm as it may influence its capital structure and stock price.

   a. Dividend puzzle
   b. Dividend yield
   c. Dividend payout ratio
   d. Dividend decision

3. _____ is the price at which an asset would trade in a competitive Walrasian auction setting. _____ is often used interchangeably with open _____, fair value or fair _____, although these terms have distinct definitions in different standards, and may differ in some circumstances.

   International Valuation Standards defines _____ as 'the estimated amount for which a property should exchange on the date of valuation between a willing buyer and a willing seller in an arm'e;s-length transaction after proper marketing wherein the parties had each acted knowledgeably, prudently, and without compulsion.'

   _____ is a concept distinct from market price, which is 'e;the price at which one can transact'e;, while _____ is 'e;the true underlying value'e; according to theoretical standards.

   a. Debt restructuring
   b. T-Model
   c. Wrap account
   d. Market value

4. A '_____' is a 'Charge' that is paid to obtain the right to delay a payment. Essentially, the payer purchases the right to make a given payment in the future instead of in the Present. The '_____', or 'Charge' that must be paid to delay the payment, is simply the difference between what the payment amount would be if it were paid in the present and what the payment amount would be paid if it were paid in the future.

   a. Risk aversion
   b. Value at risk
   c. Discount
   d. Risk modeling

5. _____ are the earnings returned on the initial investment amount.

   In the US, the Financial Accounting Standards Board (FASB) requires companies' income statements to report _____ for each of the major categories of the income statement: continuing operations, discontinued operations, extraordinary items, and net income.

   The _____ formula does not include preferred dividends for categories outside of continued operations and net income.

   a. Earnings per share
   b. Assets turnover
   c. Average accounting return
   d. Inventory turnover

Chapter 18. EARNINGS

6. In finance, _____, also known as return on investment is the ratio of money gained or lost on an investment relative to the amount of money invested. The amount of money gained or lost may be referred to as interest, profit/loss, gain/loss, or net income/loss. The money invested may be referred to as the asset, capital, principal, or the cost basis of the investment.
   a. Doctrine of the Proper Law
   b. Stock or scrip dividends
   c. Composiition of Creditors
   d. Rate of return

7. _____ measures the rate of return on the ownership interest (shareholders' equity) of the common stock owners. _____ is viewed as one of the most important financial ratios. It measures a firm's efficiency at generating profits from every dollar of shareholders' equity (also known as net assets or assets minus liabilities.)
   a. Return on equity
   b. Diluted Earnings Per Share
   c. Return of capital
   d. Return on sales

8. In business and finance, a _____ (also referred to as equity _____) of stock means a _____ of ownership in a corporation (company.) In the plural, stocks is often used as a synonym for _____s especially in the United States, but it is less commonly used that way outside of North America.

   In the United Kingdom, South Africa, and Australia, stock can also refer to completely different financial instruments such as government bonds or, less commonly, to all kinds of marketable securities.

   a. Share
   b. Bucket shop
   c. Procter ' Gamble
   d. Margin

9. _____ is the standard framework of guidelines for financial accounting used in the United States of America. It includes the standards, conventions, and rules accountants follow in recording and summarizing transactions, and in the preparation of financial statements. _____ are now issued by the Financial Accounting Standards Board (FASB).
   a. Revenue
   b. Generally accepted accounting principles
   c. Depreciation
   d. Net income

10. A _____ is a tax designation for a corporation investing in real estate that reduces or eliminates corporate income taxes. In return, _____s are required to distribute 95% of their income, which may be taxable in the hands of the investors. The _____ structure was designed to provide a similar structure for investment in real estate as mutual funds provide for investment in stocks.
    a. Liquidation value
    b. Real Estate Investment Trust
    c. Real estate investing
    d. REIT

11. In investments, _____ refers to the annual rate of growth of earnings. When the dividend payout ratio is the same, the dividend growth rate is equal to the _____ rate.

    _____ rate is a key value that is needed when the DCF model, or the Gordon's model is used for stock valuation.

    a. Annuity
    b. Earnings growth
    c. Alternative asset
    d. Alternative display facility

Chapter 18. EARNINGS

12. A _____, is a mathematical formalization of a trajectory that consists of taking successive random steps. The results of _____ analysis have been applied to computer science, physics, ecology, economics and a number of other fields as a fundamental model for random processes in time. For example, the path traced by a molecule as it travels in a liquid or a gas, the search path of a foraging animal, the price of a fluctuating stock and the financial status of a gambler can all be modeled as _____s.
    a. 529 plan
    b. 4-4-5 Calendar
    c. 7-Eleven
    d. Random walk

13. The _____ is a random-based mobility model used in mobility management schemes for mobile communication systems. The mobility model is designed to describe the movement pattern of mobile users, and how their location, velocity and acceleration change over time. Mobility models are used for simulation purposes when new network protocols are evaluated.
    a. 7-Eleven
    b. 529 plan
    c. 4-4-5 Calendar
    d. Random waypoint model

14. _____ is commonly defined as the amount of a company's or a person's income before all deductions or any taxpayer's income, except that which is specifically excluded by the Internal Revenue Code, before taking deductions or taxes into account. For a business, this amount is pre-tax net sales less cost of sales. Section 61 of the Internal Revenue Code (Code) defines '_____' as 'all income from whatever source derived.' Section 61(a) of the Code lists fifteen examples of items included in _____; however, the list is not exhaustive.
    a. Shareholder value
    b. Second lien loan
    c. Gross income
    d. Financial distress

15. The _____ is a stock exchange based in New York City, New York. It is the largest stock exchange in the world by dollar value of its listed companies securities. As of October 2008, the combined capitalization of all domestic _____ listed companies was $10.1 trillion.
    a. 7-Eleven
    b. 529 plan
    c. 4-4-5 Calendar
    d. New York Stock Exchange

16. A _____, securities exchange or (in Europe) bourse is a corporation or mutual organization which provides 'trading' facilities for stock brokers and traders, to trade stocks and other securities. _____s also provide facilities for the issue and redemption of securities as well as other financial instruments and capital events including the payment of income and dividends. The securities traded on a _____ include: shares issued by companies, unit trusts and other pooled investment products and bonds.
    a. Stock Exchange
    b. 4-4-5 Calendar
    c. 7-Eleven
    d. 529 plan

17. In finance, an _____ is the difference between the expected return of a security and the actual return. _____s are sometimes triggered by 'events.' Events can include mergers, dividend announcements, company earning announcements, interest rate increases, lawsuits, etc. all which can contribute to an _____.
    a. ABN Amro
    b. A Random Walk Down Wall Street
    c. Abnormal return
    d. AAB

18. A _____ is a fungible, negotiable instrument representing financial value. They are broadly categorized into debt securities (such as banknotes, bonds and debentures), and equity securities; e.g., common stocks. The company or other entity issuing the _____ is called the issuer.

a. Tracking stock
b. Securities lending
c. Book entry
d. Security

19. _____ and earnings management are euphemisms referring to accounting practices that may follow the letter of the rules of standard accounting practices, but certainly deviate from the spirit of those rules. They are characterized by excessive complication and the use of novel ways of characterizing income, assets, or liabilities and the intent to influence readers towards the interpretations desired by the authors. The terms 'innovative' or 'aggressive' are also sometimes used.

a. Non Performing Asset
b. Creative accounting
c. Controlling account
d. Debit and credit

20. In statistics, a _____ is the difference between the actual or real and the predicted or forecast value of a time series or any other phenomenon of interest.

In simple cases, a forecast is compared with an outcome at a single time-point and a summary of _____s is constructed over a collection of such time-points. Here the forecast may be assessed using the difference or using a proportional error.

a. Forecast error
b. 7-Eleven
c. 4-4-5 Calendar
d. 529 plan

Chapter 19. OPTIONS

1. A _____ is a financial contract between two parties, the buyer and the seller of this type of option. Often it is simply labeled a 'call'. The buyer of the option has the right, but not the obligation to buy an agreed quantity of a particular commodity or financial instrument (the underlying instrument) from the seller of the option at a certain time (the expiration date) for a certain price (the strike price.)

   a. Bull spread
   c. Call option
   b. Bear spread
   d. Bear call spread

2. In options, the _____ is a key variable in a derivatives contract between two parties. Where the contract requires delivery of the underlying instrument, the trade will be at the _____, regardless of the spot price (market price) of the underlying instrument at that time.

   Definition - The fixed price at which the owner of an option can purchase, in the case of a call in the case of a put, the underlying security or commodity.

   a. Moneyness
   c. Naked put
   b. Swaption
   d. Strike price

3. An _____ is a contract written by a seller that conveys to the buyer the right -- but not the obligation -- to buy (in the case of a call _____) or to sell (in the case of a put _____) a particular asset, such as a piece of property such as, among others, a futures contract. In return for granting the _____, the seller collects a payment (the premium) from the buyer.

   For example, buying a call _____ provides the right to buy a specified quantity of a security at a set strike price at some time on or before expiration, while buying a put _____ provides the right to sell.

   a. Amortization
   c. AT'T Mobility LLC
   b. Option
   d. Annuity

4. An _____ is defined as 'a promise which meets the requirements for the formation of a contract and limits the promisor's power to revoke an offer.' Restatement (Second) of Contracts § 25 (1981.)

   Quite simply, an _____ is a type of contract that protects an offeree from an offeror's ability to revoke the contract.

   Consideration for the _____ is still required as it is still a form of contract.

   a. ABN Amro
   c. A Random Walk Down Wall Street
   b. Option contract
   d. AAB

5. A _____ is an exchange of promises between two or more parties to do an act which is enforceable in a court of law. It is where an unqualified offer meets a qualified acceptance and the parties reach Consensus ad Idem. The parties must have the necessary capacity to _____ and the _____ must not be either trifling, indeterminate, impossible or illegal.

   a. 4-4-5 Calendar
   c. 7-Eleven
   b. 529 plan
   d. Contract

6. In finance, a _____ is a standardized contract, to buy or sell a specified commodity of standardized quality at a certain date in the future, at a market determined price (the futures price.)

The price is determined by the instantaneous equilibrium between the forces of supply and demand among competing buy and sell orders on the exchange at the time of the purchase or sale of the contract.

In many cases, the items may be such non-traditional 'commodities' as foreign currencies, commercial or government paper [e.g., bonds], or 'baskets' of corporate equity ['stock indices'] or other financial instruments.

a. Repurchase agreement
b. Futures contract
c. Heston model
d. Financial future

7. A _____ is a payment made by a corporation to its shareholder members. When a corporation earns a profit or surplus, that money can be put to two uses: it can either be re-invested in the business (called retained earnings), or it can be paid to the shareholders as a _____. Many corporations retain a portion of their earnings and pay the remainder as a _____.

a. Special dividend
b. Dividend
c. Dividend puzzle
d. Dividend yield

8. A _____ or stock divide increases or decreases the number of shares in a public company. The price is adjusted such that the before and after market capitalization of the company remains the same and dilution does not occur. Options and warrants are included.

a. Stop price
b. Stop order
c. Stock split
d. Contract for difference

9. A _____ is a financial contract between two parties, the seller (writer) and the buyer of the option. The put allows its buyer the right but not the obligation to sell a commodity or financial instrument (the underlying instrument) to the writer (seller) of the option at a certain time for a certain price (the strike price.) The writer (seller) has the obligation to purchase the underlying asset at that strike price, if the buyer exercises the option.

a. Bear call spread
b. Bear spread
c. Debit spread
d. Put option

10. In economic models, the _____ time frame assumes no fixed factors of production. Firms can enter or leave the marketplace, and the cost (and availability) of land, labor, raw materials, and capital goods can be assumed to vary. In contrast, in the short-run time frame, certain factors are assumed to be fixed, because there is not sufficient time for them to change.

a. Short-run
b. Long-run
c. 529 plan
d. 4-4-5 Calendar

11. A _____ is a fungible, negotiable instrument representing financial value. They are broadly categorized into debt securities (such as banknotes, bonds and debentures), and equity securities; e.g., common stocks. The company or other entity issuing the _____ is called the issuer.

a. Securities lending
b. Tracking stock
c. Security
d. Book entry

Chapter 19. OPTIONS

12. A _____ is a member of an exchange who is an employee of a member firm and executes orders, as agent, on the floor of the exchange for clients. The _____ receives an order via teletype machine from his firm's trading department and then proceeds to the appropriate trading post on the exchange floor. There he joins other brokers and the specialist in the security being bought or sold and executes the trade at the best competitive price available.

    a. Multivariate normal distribution
    b. Business valuation standards
    c. Case-Shiller Home Price Indices
    d. Floor broker

13. A _____ is a firm that quotes both a buy and a sell price in a financial instrument or commodity, hoping to make a profit on the bid/offer spread, or turn.

In foreign exchange trading, where most deals are conducted over-the-counter and are, therefore, completely virtual, the _____ sells to and buys from its clients. Hence, the client's loss and the spread is the _____ firm's profit, which gets thus compensated for the effort of providing liquidity in a competitive market.

    a. 4-4-5 Calendar
    b. 7-Eleven
    c. Market maker
    d. 529 plan

14. _____ is the name of a method of communication between professionals on a stock exchange or futures exchange which involves shouting and the use of hand signals to transfer information primarily about buy and sell orders. The part of the trading floor where this takes place is called a pit.

Examples of markets which use this system in the United States are the New York Mercantile Exchange, the Chicago Mercantile Exchange, the Chicago Board of Trade, and the Chicago Board Options Exchange.

    a. Intellidex
    b. Insider trading
    c. Equity investment
    d. Open outcry

15. In finance, a _____ is collateral that the holder of a position in securities, options, or futures contracts has to deposit to cover the credit risk of his counterparty (most often his broker.) This risk can arise if the holder has done any of the following:

- borrowed cash from the counterparty to buy securities or options,
- sold securities or options short, or
- entered into a futures contract.

The collateral can be in the form of cash or securities, and it is deposited in a _____ account. On U.S. futures exchanges, '_____' was formally called performance bond.

_____ buying is buying securities with cash borrowed from a broker, using other securities as collateral.

    a. Procter ' Gamble
    b. Margin
    c. Credit
    d. Share

Chapter 19. OPTIONS

16. In finance, _____ is the process of estimating the potential market value of a financial asset or liability. they can be done on assets (for example, investments in marketable securities such as stocks, options, business enterprises, or intangible assets such as patents and trademarks) or on liabilities (e.g., Bonds issued by a company.) _____s are required in many contexts including investment analysis, capital budgeting, merger and acquisition transactions, financial reporting, taxable events to determine the proper tax liability, and in litigation.
   a. Procter ' Gamble
   b. Share
   c. Valuation
   d. Margin

17. _____ is a form of corporation equity ownership represented in the securities. It is dangerous in comparison to preferred shares and some other investment options, in that in the event of bankruptcy, _____ investors receive their funds after preferred stockholders, bondholders, creditors, etc. On the other hand, common shares on average perform better than preferred shares or bonds over time.
   a. Stock split
   b. Stop-limit order
   c. Stock market bubble
   d. Common stock

18. In business and finance, a _____ (also referred to as equity _____) of stock means a _____ of ownership in a corporation (company.) In the plural, stocks is often used as a synonym for _____s especially in the United States, but it is less commonly used that way outside of North America.

    In the United Kingdom, South Africa, and Australia, stock can also refer to completely different financial instruments such as government bonds or, less commonly, to all kinds of marketable securities.

   a. Procter ' Gamble
   b. Bucket shop
   c. Share
   d. Margin

19. In finance, _____ refers to the value of a security which is intrinsic to or contained in the security itself. It is also frequently called fundamental value. It is ordinarily calculated by summing the future income generated by the asset, and discounting it to the present value.
   a. Amortization
   b. Intrinsic value
   c. Alpha
   d. Accretion

20. A _____ occurs when a speculator writes (sells) a call option on a security without ownership of that security. It is one of the riskiest options strategies because it carries unlimited risk as opposed to a naked put where the maximum loss occurs if the stock falls to zero.

    The buyer of a call option has the right to buy a specific number of shares at a strike price before an expiration date from the call option seller.

   a. Bed Bath ' Beyond Inc.
   b. Rate of return
   c. Comanity
   d. Naked call

21. A put option is a right to sell a particular stock to the writer of the option at a certain price (the strike price) on or by the expiration date. If the contract writer does not have an offsetting short position in the stock that the contract is written on, the put writer is considered uncovered for the loss incurred if the current price of the stock is below the contract price. If the writer has enough cash in his brokerage account to pay for the stock at the strike price then, although he is still considered to be in a _____ position, he may also refer more specifically to his position as a cash-covered put.

Chapter 19. OPTIONS

a. Debit spread
b. Moneyness
c. Bear put spread
d. Naked put

22. In finance, a _____ is an investment strategy involving the purchase or sale of particular option derivatives that allows the holder to profit based on how much the price of the underlying security moves, regardless of the direction of price movement. The purchase of particular option derivatives is known as a long _____, while the sale of the option derivatives is known as a short _____.

An option payoff diagram for a long _____ position

A long _____ involves going long, i.e., purchasing, both a call option and a put option on some stock, interest rate, index or other underlying.

a. Moneyness
b. Bear call spread
c. Put option
d. Straddle

23. The term _____ refers to three closely related concepts:

- The _____ model is a mathematical model of the market for an equity, in which the equity's price is a stochastic process.
- The _____ PDE is a partial differential equation which (in the model) must be satisfied by the price of a derivative on the equity.
- The _____ formula is the result obtained by solving the _____ PDE for a European call option.

Fischer Black and Myron Scholes first articulated the _____ formula in their 1973 paper, 'The Pricing of Options and Corporate Liabilities.' The foundation for their research relied on work developed by scholars such as Jack L. Treynor, Paul Samuelson, A. James Boness, Sheen T. Kassouf, and Edward O. Thorp. The fundamental insight of _____ is that the option is implicitly priced if the stock is traded.

Robert C. Merton was the first to publish a paper expanding the mathematical understanding of the options pricing model and coined the term '_____' options pricing model.

a. Modified Internal Rate of Return
b. Black-Scholes
c. Stochastic volatility
d. Perpetuity

24. A _____ is a transaction in which the seller of call options already owns the corresponding amount of the underlying instrument, such as shares of a stock or other securities. These owned shares provide the 'cover' as they can be handed over to the buyer of the options when he decides to exercise them, instead of having to buy the optioned shares at unfavorable market prices in the case of 'uncovered' or short call. Thus, the _____ limits the (potentially unlimited) loss that results from a short call when the price of the underlying stock moves above the strike price of the option.

a. 529 plan
b. 7-Eleven
c. 4-4-5 Calendar
d. Covered call

Chapter 19. OPTIONS

25. In economics and finance, _____ is the practice of taking advantage of a price differential between two or more markets: striking a combination of matching deals that capitalize upon the imbalance, the profit being the difference between the market prices. When used by academics, an _____ is a transaction that involves no negative cash flow at any probabilistic or temporal state and a positive cash flow in at least one state; in simple terms, a risk-free profit.

   a. Efficient-market hypothesis
   b. Arbitrage
   c. Initial margin
   d. Issuer

26. _____ , in finance, is a general theory of asset pricing, that has become influential in the pricing of stocks.

   _____ holds that the expected return of a financial asset can be modeled as a linear function of various macro-economic factors or theoretical market indices, where sensitivity to changes in each factor is represented by a factor-specific beta coefficient. The model-derived rate of return will then be used to price the asset correctly - the asset price should equal the expected end of period price discounted at the rate implied by model.

   a. A Random Walk Down Wall Street
   b. AAB
   c. ABN Amro
   d. Arbitrage pricing theory

27. In the valuation of a life insurance company, the actuary considers a series of future uncertain cashflows (including incoming premiums and outgoing claims, for example) and attempts to put a value on these cashflows. There are many ways of calculating such a value , but these approaches are often arbitrary in that the interest rate chosen for discounting is itself rather arbitrarily chosen.

   One possible approach, and one that is gaining increasing attention, is the use of _____ or hedge portfolios. The theory is that we can choose a portfolio of assets (fixed interest bonds, zero coupon bonds, index-linked bonds, etc.) whose cashflows are identical to the magnitude and the timing of the cashflows to be valued.

   a. 7-Eleven
   b. Replicating portfolios
   c. 529 plan
   d. 4-4-5 Calendar

28. In finance, _____ or 'shorting' is the practice of selling a financial instrument that the seller does not own at the time of the sale. _____ is done with intent of later purchasing the financial instrument at a lower price. Short-sellers attempt to profit from an expected decline in the price of a financial instrument.

   a. 4-4-5 Calendar
   b. Short selling
   c. 529 plan
   d. Short ratio

29. In finance, a _____ is a position established in one market in an attempt to offset exposure to the price risk of an equal but opposite obligation or position in another market -- usually, but not always, in the context of one's commercial activity. Hedging is a strategy designed to minimize exposure to such business risks as a sharp contraction in demand for one's inventory, while still allowing the business to profit from producing and maintaining that inventory. A typical hedger might be a farmer with 2000 acres of unharvested wheat in the ground, who would rather tend his crop without the distraction of uncertain prices.

   a. 4-4-5 Calendar
   b. 529 plan
   c. Hedge
   d. 7-Eleven

Chapter 19. OPTIONS

30. In financial mathematics, _____ defines a relationship between the price of a call option and a put option--both with the identical strike price and expiry. To derive the _____ relationship, the assumption is that the options are not exercised before expiration day, which necessarily applies to European options. _____ can be derived in a manner that is largely model independent.
   a. Cox-Ingersoll-Ross model
   b. Hull-White model
   c. Rendleman-Bartter model
   d. Put-call parity

31. _____, static projection, and static scoring are pejorative terms for statistical analyses for which existing trends are projected into the future simplistically, or beyond what is possible to predict in any manner, producing results often wildly unrealistic.

   Its opposite, dynamic analysis or dynamic scoring, is an attempt to take into account how variables may change or interact. One common use of these terms is budget policy in the United States, although it also occurs in many other statistical disputes.

   a. 4-4-5 Calendar
   b. 529 plan
   c. 7-Eleven
   d. Static analysis

32. _____ most frequently refers to the standard deviation of the continuously compounded returns of a financial instrument with a specific time horizon. It is often used to quantify the risk of the instrument over that time period. _____ is typically expressed in annualized terms, and it may either be an absolute number ($5) or a fraction of the mean (5%).
   a. Volatility
   b. Currency swap
   c. Portfolio insurance
   d. Seasoned equity offering

33. In financial mathematics, the _____ of an option contract is the volatility implied by the market price of the option based on an option pricing model. In other words, it is the volatility that, given a particular pricing model, yields a theoretical value for the option equal to the current market price. Non-option financial instruments that have embedded optionality, such as an interest rate cap, can also have an _____.
   a. Interest rate derivative
   b. Interest rate future
   c. Implied volatility
   d. Equity derivative

34. In finance, the value of an option consists of two components, its intrinsic value and its _____. Time value is simply the difference between option value and intrinsic value. _____ is also known as theta, extrinsic value, or instrumental value.
   a. Conservatism
   b. Global Squeeze
   c. Time value
   d. Debt buyer

35. _____ means regulating, adapting or settling in a variety of contexts:

   In commercial law, _____ means the settlement of a loss incurred on insured goods. The calculation of the amounts of compensation to be paid by or to the several interests is a complicated matter. It involves much detail and arithmetic, and requires a full and accurate knowledge of the principles of the subject.

   a. Equity method
   b. Adjustment
   c. Asset recovery
   d. Intelligent investor

Chapter 19. OPTIONS

36. _____ is a method of hedging a portfolio of stocks against the market risk by short selling stock index futures.

This hedging technique is frequently used by institutional investors when the market direction is uncertain or volatile. Short selling index futures can offset any downturns, but it also hinders any gains.

a. PAUG
b. Delivery month
c. Portfolio insurance
d. Freight derivative

37. _____ refers to a business or organization attempting to acquire goods or services to accomplish the goals of the enterprise. Though there are several organizations that attempt to set standards in the _____ process, processes can vary greatly between organizations. Typically the word '_____' is not used interchangeably with the word 'procurement', since procurement typically includes Expediting, Supplier Quality, and Traffic and Logistics (T'L) in addition to _____.

a. 529 plan
b. 4-4-5 Calendar
c. 7-Eleven
d. Purchasing

38. _____ is the difference between price and the costs of bringing to market whatever it is that is accounted as an enterprise (whether by harvest, extraction, manufacture, or purchase) in terms of the component costs of delivered goods and/or services and any operating or other expenses.

A key difficulty in measuring profit is in defining costs. Pure economic monetary profits can be zero or negative even in competitive equilibrium when accounted monetized costs exceed monetized price.

a. Economic profit
b. Accounting profit
c. AAB
d. A Random Walk Down Wall Street

39. _____ is casually defined as the use of computers in stock markets to engage in arbitrage and portfolio insurance strategies. However, the New York Stock Exchange (NYSE) defines the term as 'a wide range of portfolio trading strategies involving the purchase or sale of 15 or more stocks having a total market value of $1 million or more' without any direct reference to the use of computers. The word 'program' can be interpreted in its earlier, more general meaning of a defined and pre-arranged sequence of steps, rather than specifically a computer program.

a. Wash sale
b. Program trading
c. Share price
d. Stop order

40. In finance, a _____ is a security that entitles the holder to buy stock of the company that issued it at a specified price, which is usually higher than the stock price at time of issue.

_____s are frequently attached to bonds or preferred stock as a sweetener, allowing the issuer to pay lower interest rates or dividends. They can be used to enhance the yield of the bond, and make them more attractive to potential buyers.

a. Credit
b. Clearing
c. Clearing house
d. Warrant

41. In finance, a _____ is a debt security, in which the authorized issuer owes the holders a debt and, depending on the terms of the _____, is obliged to pay interest (the coupon) and/or to repay the principal at a later date, termed maturity.

Thus a _____ is a loan: the issuer is the borrower, the _____ holder is the lender, and the coupon is the interest. _____s provide the borrower with external funds to finance long-term investments, or, in the case of government _____s, to finance current expenditure.

a. Puttable bond
c. Bond

b. Catastrophe bonds
d. Convertible bond

42. In finance, a _____ is a type of bond that can be converted into shares of stock in the issuing company, usually at some pre-announced ratio. It is a hybrid security with debt- and equity-like features. Although it typically has a low coupon rate, the holder is compensated with the ability to convert the bond to common stock, usually at a substantial discount to the stock's market value.

a. Bond fund
c. Corporate bond

b. Convertible bond
d. Gilts

43. In financial accounting, _____s are precautions for which the amount or probability of occurrence are not known. Typical examples are _____s for warranty costs and _____ for taxes the term reserve is used instead of term _____; such a use, however, is inconsistent with the terminology suggested by International Accounting Standards Board.

a. Petty cash
c. Money measurement concept

b. Momentum Accounting and Triple-Entry Bookkeeping
d. Provision

Chapter 20. FUTURES

1. In finance, a _____ is a standardized contract, to buy or sell a specified commodity of standardized quality at a certain date in the future, at a market determined price (the futures price.)

The price is determined by the instantaneous equilibrium between the forces of supply and demand among competing buy and sell orders on the exchange at the time of the purchase or sale of the contract.

In many cases, the items may be such non-traditional 'commodities' as foreign currencies, commercial or government paper [e.g., bonds], or 'baskets' of corporate equity ['stock indices'] or other financial instruments.

   a. Futures contract
   b. Heston model
   c. Financial future
   d. Repurchase agreement

2. In finance, a _____ is a position established in one market in an attempt to offset exposure to the price risk of an equal but opposite obligation or position in another market -- usually, but not always, in the context of one's commercial activity. Hedging is a strategy designed to minimize exposure to such business risks as a sharp contraction in demand for one's inventory, while still allowing the business to profit from producing and maintaining that inventory. A typical hedger might be a farmer with 2000 acres of unharvested wheat in the ground, who would rather tend his crop without the distraction of uncertain prices.

   a. 4-4-5 Calendar
   b. Hedge
   c. 7-Eleven
   d. 529 plan

3. The _____ or cash market is a commodities or securities market in which goods are sold for cash and delivered immediately. Contracts bought and sold on these markets are immediately effective. _____s can operate wherever the infrastructure exists to conduct the transaction.

   a. Currency swap
   b. Non-deliverable forward
   c. Foreign exchange controls
   d. Spot market

4. The _____ or spot rate of a commodity, a security or a currency is the price that is quoted for immediate (spot) settlement (payment and delivery.) Spot settlement is normally one or two business days from trade date. This is in contrast with the forward price established in a forward contract or futures contract, where contract terms (price) are set now, but delivery and payment will occur at a future date.

   a. Spot price
   b. Market price
   c. Cost of carry
   d. Central Securities Depository

5. A _____ is an exchange of promises between two or more parties to do an act which is enforceable in a court of law. It is where an unqualified offer meets a qualified acceptance and the parties reach Consensus ad Idem. The parties must have the necessary capacity to _____ and the _____ must not be either trifling, indeterminate, impossible or illegal.

   a. 529 plan
   b. 4-4-5 Calendar
   c. Contract
   d. 7-Eleven

6. _____ denotes the total number of derivative contracts, like futures and options, that are currently active on a specific underlying security, having specific terms.

Chapter 20. FUTURES

Namely, the total contracts for a specific strike price and expiration date, that have been traded, but have not yet expired, have not yet been closed through a closing transaction, or have not yet been terminated via early exercise. A closing transaction occurs when a counterparty that longs the contract sells, or, conversely, when a counterparty that shorts the contract buys.

a. International Swaps and Derivatives Association
b. Equity derivative
c. Equity swap
d. Open interest

7. _____ is a fee paid on borrowed assets. It is the price paid for the use of borrowed money, or, money earned by deposited funds. Assets that are sometimes lent with _____ include money, shares, consumer goods through hire purchase, major assets such as aircraft, and even entire factories in finance lease arrangements.
a. AAB
b. Insolvency
c. A Random Walk Down Wall Street
d. Interest

8. An _____ is a contract written by a seller that conveys to the buyer the right -- but not the obligation -- to buy (in the case of a call _____) or to sell (in the case of a put _____) a particular asset, such as a piece of property such as, among others, a futures contract. In return for granting the _____, the seller collects a payment (the premium) from the buyer.

For example, buying a call _____ provides the right to buy a specified quantity of a security at a set strike price at some time on or before expiration, while buying a put _____ provides the right to sell.

a. AT'T Mobility LLC
b. Annuity
c. Amortization
d. Option

9. A _____ is a financial services company that provides clearing and settlement services for financial transactions, usually on a futures exchange, and often acts as central counterparty (the payor actually pays the _____, which then pays the payee). A _____ may also offer novation, the substitution of a new contract or debt for an old, or other credit enhancement services to its members.

The term is also used for banks like Suffolk Bank that acted as a restraint on the over-issuance of private bank notes.

a. Warrant
b. Clearing house
c. Bucket shop
d. Valuation

10. The _____ requirement is the amount required to be collateralized in order to open a position. Thereafter, the amount required to be kept in collateral until the position is closed is the maintenance requirement. The maintenance requirement is the minimum amount to be collateralized in order to keep an open position.
a. Issuer
b. Arbitrage
c. Efficient-market hypothesis
d. Initial margin

11. The _____ is the amount required to be collateralized in order to open a position. Thereafter, the amount required to be kept in collateral until the position is closed is the maintenance requirement. The maintenance requirement is the minimum amount to be collateralized in order to keep an open position.

Chapter 20. FUTURES

a. A Random Walk Down Wall Street
b. Initial margin requirement
c. ABN Amro
d. AAB

12. In finance, a _____ is collateral that the holder of a position in securities, options, or futures contracts has to deposit to cover the credit risk of his counterparty (most often his broker.) This risk can arise if the holder has done any of the following:

- borrowed cash from the counterparty to buy securities or options,
- sold securities or options short, or
- entered into a futures contract.

The collateral can be in the form of cash or securities, and it is deposited in a _____ account. On U.S. futures exchanges, '_____' was formally called performance bond.

_____ buying is buying securities with cash borrowed from a broker, using other securities as collateral.

a. Procter ' Gamble
b. Credit
c. Share
d. Margin

13. The variation margin or _____ is not collateral, but a daily offsetting of profits and losses. Futures are marked-to-market every day, so the current price is compared to the previous day's price. The profit or loss on the day of a position is then paid to or debited from the holder by the futures exchange.

a. Total return swap
b. Delivery month
c. SPI 200 futures contract
d. Maintenance margin

14. A _____ is something for which there is demand, but which is supplied without qualitative differentiation across a market. It is a product that is the same no matter who produces it, such as petroleum, notebook paper, or milk. In other words, copper is copper.

a. 7-Eleven
b. 4-4-5 Calendar
c. 529 plan
d. Commodity

15. _____ in finance is the risk associated with imperfect hedging using futures. It could arise because of the difference between the asset whose price is to be hedged and the asset underlying the derivative, or because of a mismatch between the expiration date of the futures and the actual selling date of the asset.

Under these conditions, the spot price of the asset, and the futures price, do not converge on the expiration date of the future.

a. Credit risk
b. Currency risk
c. Liquidity risk
d. Basis risk

16. In the context of financial futures, _____ can be defined as the spot price minus the futures price. There will be a different basis for each delivery month for each contract. In a normal market, basis will be negative.

a. Municipal Okrug #7
b. Controlled foreign corporations
c. Legal and regulatory risk
d. Basis of futures

Chapter 20. FUTURES

17. A _____ is a measure of the average price of consumer goods and services purchased by households. The _____ can be used to index (i.e., adjust for the effects of inflation) wages, salaries, pensions, or regulated or contracted prices. The _____ is, along with the population census and the National Income and Product Accounts, one of the most closely watched national economic statistics.

    a. 529 plan
    b. Consumer Price Index
    c. 4-4-5 Calendar
    d. Divisia index

18. A _____ is a normalized average (typically a weighted average) of prices for a given class of goods or services in a given region, during a given interval of time. It is a statistic designed to help to compare how these prices, taken as a whole, differ between time periods or geographical locations.

    a. Price discrimination
    b. Transfer pricing
    c. Discounts and allowances
    d. Price Index

19. _____ is a futures market term. It describes a situation where the amount of money required for future delivery of an item is lower than the amount required for immediate delivery of that item. For example, immediate delivery of gold may cost $1,000 an ounce, whereas delivery in two months only costs $900 an ounce, with that $900 to be paid at time of delivery.

    a. Risk-neutral measure
    b. STIRT
    c. Delivery month
    d. Backwardation

20. _____ is a term used in the futures market to describe an upward sloping forward curve (as in the normal yield curve.) Such a forward curve is said to be 'in _____' (or sometimes '_____ed'.)

Formally, it is the situation where, and the amount by which, the price of a commodity for future delivery is higher than the spot price, or a far future delivery price higher than a nearer future delivery.

    a. Single-stock futures
    b. Delta One
    c. Commodity tick
    d. Contango

21. A _____ is an adjustment to the cost of carry in the non-arbitrage pricing formula for forward prices in markets with trading constraints.

Let $F_{t,T}$ be the forward price of an asset with initial price S_t and maturity T. Suppose that r is the continuously compounded interest rate for one year. Then, the non-arbitrage pricing formula should be

$F_{t,T} = S_t e^{r(T >- t)}$.

    a. 7-Eleven
    b. 4-4-5 Calendar
    c. Convenience yield
    d. 529 plan

22. In economics, business, and accounting, a _____ is the value of money that has been used up to produce something, and hence is not available for use anymore. In business, the _____ may be one of acquisition, in which case the amount of money expended to acquire it is counted as _____. In this case, money is the input that is gone in order to acquire the thing.

a. Marginal cost
b. Cost
c. Sliding scale fees
d. Fixed costs

23. The _____ is the cost of 'carrying' or holding a position. If long, the _____ is the cost of interest paid on a margin account. Conversely, if short, the _____ is the cost of paying dividends, or opportunity cost the cost of purchasing a particular security rather than an alternative.

   a. Secondary market
   b. Spot price
   c. Delta hedging
   d. Cost of carry

24. A _____ is a futures contract on a short term interest rate (STIR.) Contracts vary, but are often defined on an interest rate index such as 3-month sterling or US dollar LIBOR.

   They are traded across a wide range of currencies, including the G12 country currencies and many others.

   a. Dual currency deposit
   b. Notional amount
   c. Real estate derivatives
   d. Financial future

25. In finance, the term _____ describes the amount in cash that returns to the owners of a security. Normally it does not include the price variations, at the difference of the total return. _____ applies to various stated rates of return on stocks (common and preferred, and convertible), fixed income instruments (bonds, notes, bills, strips, zero coupon), and some other investment type insurance products (e.g. annuities.)

   a. 4-4-5 Calendar
   b. Macaulay duration
   c. Yield
   d. Yield to maturity

26. In finance, a _____ is a debt security, in which the authorized issuer owes the holders a debt and, depending on the terms of the _____, is obliged to pay interest (the coupon) and/or to repay the principal at a later date, termed maturity.

   Thus a _____ is a loan: the issuer is the borrower, the _____ holder is the lender, and the coupon is the interest. _____s provide the borrower with external funds to finance long-term investments, or, in the case of government _____s, to finance current expenditure.

   a. Puttable bond
   b. Convertible bond
   c. Catastrophe bonds
   d. Bond

27. The _____ of an asset is the return obtained from holding it (if positive), or the cost of holding it (if negative)

   For instance, commodities are usually negative _____ assets, as they incur storage costs, but in some circumstances, commodities can be positive _____ assets as the market is willing to pay a premium for availability.

   This can also refer to a trade with more than one leg, where you earn the spread between borrowing a low _____ asset and lending a high _____ one.

Chapter 20. FUTURES

a. Bankruptcy remote
b. Cramdown
c. Financial assistance
d. Carry

28. A _____, also FX future or foreign exchange future, is a futures contract to exchange one currency for another at a specified date in the future at a price (exchange rate) that is fixed on the purchase date. Typically, one of the currencies is the US dollar. The price of a future is then in terms of US dollars per unit of other currency.
   a. Foreign exchange controls
   b. Non-deliverable forward
   c. Currency swap
   d. Currency future

29. In the original and simplified sense, _____ were things of value, of uniform quality, that were produced in large quantities by many different producers; the items from each different producer are considered equivalent. It is the contract and this underlying standard that define the commodity, not any quality inherent in the product.

_____ exchanges include:

- Chicago Board of Trade
- Kansas City Board of Trade
- Euronext.liffe
- Kuala Lumpur Futures Exchange
- Bhatinda Om ' Oil Exchange
- London Metal Exchange
- New York Mercantile Exchange
- Multi Commodity Exchange
- Dalian Commodity Exchange

Markets for trading _____ can be very efficient, particularly if the division into pools matches demand segments. These markets will quickly respond to changes in supply and demand to find an equilibrium price and quantity.

   a. 7-Eleven
   b. 529 plan
   c. 4-4-5 Calendar
   d. Commodities

30. The _____ serves as a benchmark for investment in the commodity markets and as a measure of commodity performance over time. It is a tradable index that is readily available to market participants of the Chicago Mercantile Exchange. The index was originally developed by Goldman Sachs.
   a. 529 plan
   b. 7-Eleven
   c. 4-4-5 Calendar
   d. S'P GSCI

31. The _____ , largely the creation of Leo Melamed, is part of the Chicago Mercantile Exchange (CME), the largest futures exchange in the United States and the second largest in the world after Eurex, for the trading of futures contracts and options on futures. The _____ was started on May 16, 1972. Two of the more prevalent contracts traded are currency futures and interest rate futures.
   a. International Monetary Market
   b. ABN Amro
   c. A Random Walk Down Wall Street
   d. AAB

32. _____ refers to any type of investment that yields a regular (or fixed) return.

For example, if you lend money to a borrower and the borrower has to pay interest once a month, you have been issued a fixed-income security. When a company does this, it is often called a bond or corporate bank debt (although preferred stock is also sometimes considered to be _____).

a. 529 plan
c. Bond market
b. Fixed Income
d. 4-4-5 Calendar

33. _____, refers to consumption opportunity gained by an entity within a specified time frame, which is generally expressed in monetary terms. However, for households and individuals, '_____ is the sum of all the wages, salaries, profits, interests payments, rents and other forms of earnings received... in a given period of time.' For firms, _____ generally refers to net-profit: what remains of revenue after expenses have been subtracted.

a. OIBDA
c. Annual report
b. Accrual
d. Income

34. In economics and finance, _____ is the practice of taking advantage of a price differential between two or more markets: striking a combination of matching deals that capitalize upon the imbalance, the profit being the difference between the market prices. When used by academics, an _____ is a transaction that involves no negative cash flow at any probabilistic or temporal state and a positive cash flow in at least one state; in simple terms, a risk-free profit.

a. Efficient-market hypothesis
c. Issuer
b. Initial margin
d. Arbitrage

35. _____ is the difference between price and the costs of bringing to market whatever it is that is accounted as an enterprise (whether by harvest, extraction, manufacture, or purchase) in terms of the component costs of delivered goods and/or services and any operating or other expenses.

A key difficulty in measuring profit is in defining costs. Pure economic monetary profits can be zero or negative even in competitive equilibrium when accounted monetized costs exceed monetized price.

a. Economic profit
c. A Random Walk Down Wall Street
b. AAB
d. Accounting profit

36. _____ is casually defined as the use of computers in stock markets to engage in arbitrage and portfolio insurance strategies. However, the New York Stock Exchange (NYSE) defines the term as 'a wide range of portfolio trading strategies involving the purchase or sale of 15 or more stocks having a total market value of $1 million or more' without any direct reference to the use of computers. The word 'program' can be interpreted in its earlier, more general meaning of a defined and pre-arranged sequence of steps, rather than specifically a computer program.

a. Program trading
c. Wash sale
b. Share price
d. Stop order

37. _____ is a risk-adjusted measure of the so-called active return on an investment. It is the return in excess of the compensation for the risk borne, and thus commonly used to assess active managers' performances. Often, the return of a benchmark is subtracted in order to consider relative performance, which yields Jensen's _____.

Chapter 20. FUTURES

a. Amortization
b. Annuity
c. Alpha
d. Option

38. In business and accounting, _____s are everything of value that is owned by a person or company. The balance sheet of a firm records the monetary value of the _____s owned by the firm. The two major _____ classes are tangible _____s and intangible _____s.
   a. Income
   b. EBITDA
   c. Accounts payable
   d. Asset

39. _____ is a term used to refer to how an investor distributes his or her investments among various classes of investment vehicles (e.g., stocks and bonds.)

A large part of financial planning is finding an _____ that is appropriate for a given person in terms of their appetite for and ability to shoulder risk. This can depend on various factors; see investor profile.

   a. Alternative investment
   b. Asset allocation
   c. Investment performance
   d. Investing online

40. A _____ is a financial contract between two parties, the buyer and the seller of this type of option. Often it is simply labeled a 'call'. The buyer of the option has the right, but not the obligation to buy an agreed quantity of a particular commodity or financial instrument (the underlying instrument) from the seller of the option at a certain time (the expiration date) for a certain price (the strike price.)
   a. Bull spread
   b. Call option
   c. Bear spread
   d. Bear call spread

41. A _____ is a financial contract between two parties, the seller (writer) and the buyer of the option. The put allows its buyer the right but not the obligation to sell a commodity or financial instrument (the underlying instrument) to the writer (seller) of the option at a certain time for a certain price (the strike price.) The writer (seller) has the obligation to purchase the underlying asset at that strike price, if the buyer exercises the option.
   a. Put option
   b. Bear spread
   c. Bear call spread
   d. Debit spread

Chapter 21. INVESTMENT COMPANIES

1. An _____ is a company whose main business is holding securities of other companies purely for investment purposes. The _____ invests money on behalf of its shareholders who in turn share in the profits and losses.
   a. Unit investment trust
   b. Investment company
   c. AAB
   d. A Random Walk Down Wall Street

2. _____ is a term used to describe the value of an entity's assets less the value of its liabilities. The term is commonly used in relation to collective investment schemes. It may also be used as a synonym for the book value of a firm.
   a. Passive management
   b. Retail broker
   c. Financial intermediary
   d. Net asset value

3. A _____ is a US investment company offering a fixed (unmanaged) portfolio of securities having a definite life. _____s are assembled by a sponsor and sold through brokers to investors.

   A _____ portfolio may contain one of several different types of securities.

   a. AAB
   b. A Random Walk Down Wall Street
   c. Investment company
   d. Unit investment trust

4. In business and accounting, _____s are everything of value that is owned by a person or company. The balance sheet of a firm records the monetary value of the _____s owned by the firm. The two major _____ classes are tangible _____s and intangible _____s.
   a. Income
   b. Asset
   c. Accounts payable
   d. EBITDA

5. The _____ is the financial market where previously issued securities and financial instruments such as stock, bonds, options, and futures are bought and sold. The term '_____' is also used refer to the market for any used goods or assets, or an alternative use for an existing product or asset where the customer base is the second market

   With primary issuances of securities or financial instruments, or the primary market, investors purchase these securities directly from issuers such as corporations issuing shares in an IPO or private placement, or directly from the federal government in the case of treasuries.

   a. Financial market
   b. Performance attribution
   c. Delta neutral
   d. Secondary market

6. An _____, operating expenditure, operational expense, operational expenditure or OPEX is an on-going cost for running a product, business, or system. Its counterpart, a capital expenditure (CAPEX), is the cost of developing or providing non-consumable parts for the product or system. For example, the purchase of a photocopier is the CAPEX, and the annual paper and toner cost is the OPEX.
   a. AAB
   b. ABN Amro
   c. Operating expense
   d. A Random Walk Down Wall Street

7. A _____ is a professionally managed type of collective investment scheme that pools money from many investors and invests it in stocks, bonds, short-term money market instruments, and/or other securities. The _____ will have a fund manager that trades the pooled money on a regular basis. Currently, the worldwide value of all _____s totals more than $26 trillion.

Chapter 21. INVESTMENT COMPANIES

Since 1940, there have been three basic types of investment companies in the United States: open-end funds, also known in the US as _____s; unit investment trusts (UITs); and closed-end funds.

a. Trust company
b. Net asset value
c. Financial intermediary
d. Mutual fund

8. _____, in accrual accounting, is any account where the asset or liability is not realized until a future date, e.g. annuities, charges, taxes, income, etc. The _____ item may be carried, dependent on type of deferral, as either an asset or liability. See also: accrual

_____ is also used in the university admissions process. It is the action by which a school rejects a student for early admission but still opts to review that student in the general admissions pool.

a. Revenue
b. Deferred
c. Current asset
d. Net profit

9. _____ also known as Deferred Sales Charge, is a fee paid when shares are sold. This fee typically goes to the brokers that sell the fund's shares. The amount of this type of load will depend on how long the investor holds his or her shares and typically decreases to zero if the investor holds his or her shares long enough.

a. Money market funds
b. Back-end load
c. Closed-end fund
d. Mutual fund fees and expenses

10. In finance, a _____ is a debt security, in which the authorized issuer owes the holders a debt and, depending on the terms of the _____, is obliged to pay interest (the coupon) and/or to repay the principal at a later date, termed maturity.

Thus a _____ is a loan: the issuer is the borrower, the _____ holder is the lender, and the coupon is the interest. _____s provide the borrower with external funds to finance long-term investments, or, in the case of government _____s, to finance current expenditure.

a. Bond
b. Convertible bond
c. Puttable bond
d. Catastrophe bonds

11. A _____ is a collective investment scheme that invests in bonds and other debt securities. _____s yield monthly dividends that include interest payments on the fund's underlying securities plus any capital appreciation in the prices of the portfolio's bonds. _____s tend to pay higher dividends than CDs and money market accounts, and they generally pay out dividends more frequently and regularly than individual bonds.

a. Bond fund
b. Private activity bond
c. Premium bond
d. Gilts

12. _____ refers to any type of investment that yields a regular (or fixed) return.

For example, if you lend money to a borrower and the borrower has to pay interest once a month, you have been issued a fixed-income security. When a company does this, it is often called a bond or corporate bank debt (although preferred stock is also sometimes considered to be _____).

Chapter 21. INVESTMENT COMPANIES

   a. 529 plan
   b. 4-4-5 Calendar
   c. Bond market
   d. Fixed income

13. An _____ is any government regulation or law that encourages or discourages foreign investment in the local economy, e.g. currency exchange limits.

As globalization integrates the economies of neighboring and of trading states, they are typically forced to trade off such rules as part of a common tax, tariff and trade regime, e.g. as defined by a free trade pact. _____ favoring local investors over global ones is typically discouraged in such pacts, and the idea of a separate _____ rapidly becomes a fiction or fantasy, as real decisions reflect the real need for nations to compete for investment, even from their own local investors.

   a. ABN Amro
   b. AAB
   c. A Random Walk Down Wall Street
   d. Investment policy

14. A _____ is a fungible, negotiable instrument representing financial value. They are broadly categorized into debt securities (such as banknotes, bonds and debentures), and equity securities; e.g., common stocks. The company or other entity issuing the _____ is called the issuer.
   a. Securities lending
   b. Security
   c. Tracking stock
   d. Book entry

15. _____ is a term used to refer to how an investor distributes his or her investments among various classes of investment vehicles (e.g., stocks and bonds.)

A large part of financial planning is finding an _____ that is appropriate for a given person in terms of their appetite for and ability to shoulder risk. This can depend on various factors; see investor profile.

   a. Alternative investment
   b. Investing online
   c. Investment performance
   d. Asset allocation

16. An _____ or index tracker is a collective investment scheme (usually a mutual fund or exchange-traded fund) that aims to replicate the movements of an index of a specific financial market regardless of market conditions.

Tracking can be achieved by trying to hold all of the securities in the index, in the same proportions as the index. Other methods include statistically sampling the market and holding 'representative' securities.

   a. AAB
   b. Index fund
   c. Investment company
   d. A Random Walk Down Wall Street

17. _____, refers to consumption opportunity gained by an entity within a specified time frame, which is generally expressed in monetary terms. However, for households and individuals, '_____ is the sum of all the wages, salaries, profits, interests payments, rents and other forms of earnings received... in a given period of time.' For firms, _____ generally refers to net-profit: what remains of revenue after expenses have been subtracted.
   a. OIBDA
   b. Accrual
   c. Annual report
   d. Income

Chapter 21. INVESTMENT COMPANIES

18. _____ is a risk-adjusted measure of the so-called active return on an investment. It is the return in excess of the compensation for the risk borne, and thus commonly used to assess active managers' performances. Often, the return of a benchmark is subtracted in order to consider relative performance, which yields Jensen's _____.
   a. Alpha
   b. Amortization
   c. Option
   d. Annuity

19. In economics and finance, _____ is the practice of taking advantage of a price differential between two or more markets: striking a combination of matching deals that capitalize upon the imbalance, the profit being the difference between the market prices. When used by academics, an _____ is a transaction that involves no negative cash flow at any probabilistic or temporal state and a positive cash flow in at least one state; in simple terms, a risk-free profit.
   a. Efficient-market hypothesis
   b. Initial margin
   c. Arbitrage
   d. Issuer

20. A _____ is a method of measuring a section of the stock market. Many indices are cited by news or financial services firms and are used to benchmark the performance of portfolios such as mutual funds.
   a. Trading curb
   b. Program trading
   c. Stop order
   d. Stock market index

21. A _____ or equity fund is a fund that invests in Equities more commonly known as stocks. Such funds are typically held either in stock or cash, as opposed to Bonds, notes, or other securities. This may be a mutual fund or exchange-traded fund.
   a. Stock fund
   b. Money market funds
   c. Closed-end fund
   d. Mutual fund fees and expenses

22. _____ refers to different style characteristics of equities, bonds or financial derivatives within a given investment philosophy.

Theory would favor a combination of big capitalization, passive and value. Of course one could almost get that when investing in an important Index like S'P 500, Euro-Stoxx or the like.

   a. AAB
   b. Investment style
   c. ABN Amro
   d. A Random Walk Down Wall Street

23. A _____, is a collective investment scheme with a limited number of shares.

New shares are rarely issued after the fund is launched; shares are not normally redeemable for cash or securities until the fund liquidates. Typically an investor can acquire shares in a _____ by buying shares on a secondary market from a broker, market maker, or other investor as opposed to an open-end fund where all transactions eventually involve the fund company creating new shares on the fly (in exchange for either cash or securities) or redeeming shares (for cash or securities.)

   a. Closed-end fund
   b. Stock fund
   c. Money market funds
   d. Mutual fund fees and expenses

Chapter 21. INVESTMENT COMPANIES

24. In business and finance, a _____ (also referred to as equity _____) of stock means a _____ of ownership in a corporation (company.) In the plural, stocks is often used as a synonym for _____s especially in the United States, but it is less commonly used that way outside of North America.

In the United Kingdom, South Africa, and Australia, stock can also refer to completely different financial instruments such as government bonds or, less commonly, to all kinds of marketable securities.

    a. Share
    b. Procter ' Gamble
    c. Bucket shop
    d. Margin

25. A _____ or _____ is a tax designation for a corporation investing in real estate that reduces or eliminates corporate income taxes. In return, _____s are required to distribute 95% of their income, which may be taxable in the hands of the investors. The _____ structure was designed to provide a similar structure for investment in real estate as mutual funds provide for investment in stocks.

    a. Liquidation value
    b. Tenancy
    c. Real estate investing
    d. Real estate investment trust

Chapter 22. FINANCIAL ANALYSIS

1. _____ is an international professional designation offered by the _____ Institute (formerly known as AIMR) to financial analysts who complete a series of three examinations. In order to become a '_____ Charterholder' candidates must pass all three six-hour exams, possess a bachelor's degree (or equivalent, as assessed by the _____ institute) and have 48 months of work experience in an investment decision-making position. _____ charterholders are also obligated to adhere to a strict Code of Ethics and Standards governing their professional conduct.
   a. Chartered Financial Analyst
   b. 4-4-5 Calendar
   c. 7-Eleven
   d. 529 plan

2. The institution most often referenced by the word '_____' is a public or publicly traded _____, the shares of which are traded on a public stock exchange (e.g., the New York Stock Exchange or Nasdaq in the United States) where shares of stock of _____s are bought and sold by and to the general public. Most of the largest businesses in the world are publicly traded _____s. However, the majority of _____s are said to be closely held, privately held or close _____s, meaning that no ready market exists for the trading of shares.
   a. Depository Trust Company
   b. Federal Home Loan Mortgage Corporation
   c. Corporation
   d. Protect

3. The _____ (NYSE: FRE) is an insolvent government sponsored enterprise (GSE) of the United States federal government.

The _____ was created in 1970 to expand the secondary market for mortgages in the US. Along with other GSEs, Freddie Mac buys mortgages on the secondary market, pools them, and sells them as mortgage-backed securities to investors on the open market.

   a. Public company
   b. Governmental Accounting Standards Board
   c. The Depository Trust ' Clearing Corporation
   d. Federal Home Loan Mortgage Corporation

4. A _____, securities analyst, research analyst, equity analyst, or investment analyst is a person who performs financial analysis for external or internal clients as a core part of the job.

An analyst studies companies and other entities to arrive at the estimate of their financial value. It is normally done by analyzing financial reports, aided by follow-up interviews with company representatives and industry experts.

   a. Financial Analyst
   b. Stockbroker
   c. Purchasing manager
   d. Portfolio manager

5. _____ refers to an assessment of the viability, stability and profitability of a business, sub-business or project.

It is performed by professionals who prepare reports using ratios that make use of information taken from financial statements and other reports. These reports are usually presented to top management as one of their bases in making business decisions.

   a. 529 plan
   b. 4-4-5 Calendar
   c. Value investing
   d. Financial analysis

6. _____ of a business involves analyzing its financial statements and health, its management and competitive advantages, and its competitors and markets. The term is used to distinguish such analysis from other types of investment analysis, such as quantitative analysis and technical analysis.

Chapter 22. FINANCIAL ANALYSIS

_____ is performed on historical and present data, but with the goal of making financial forecasts.

a. 4-4-5 Calendar
b. Fundamental analysis
c. Stock valuation
d. Growth stocks

7. A _____ is a person who makes investment decisions using money other people have placed under his or her control. In other words, it is a financial career involved in investment management. They work with a team of analysts and researchers, and are ultimately responsible for establishing an investment strategy, selecting appropriate investments and allocating each investment properly for a fund- or asset-management vehicle.

a. Day trader
b. Financial analyst
c. Purchasing manager
d. Portfolio manager

8. A _____ is a fungible, negotiable instrument representing financial value. They are broadly categorized into debt securities (such as banknotes, bonds and debentures), and equity securities; e.g., common stocks. The company or other entity issuing the _____ is called the issuer.

a. Tracking stock
b. Securities lending
c. Book entry
d. Security

9. _____ is a security analysis discipline for forecasting the future direction of prices through the study of past market data, primarily price and volume. In its purest form, _____ considers only the actual price and volume behavior of the market or instrument. Technical analysts may employ models and trading rules based on price and volume transformations, such as the relative strength index, moving averages, regressions, inter-market and intra-market price correlations, cycles or, classically, through recognition of chart patterns.

a. Technical analysis
b. Point and figure
c. Support and resistance
d. Dow theory

10. In finance, a _____ is one who attempts to profit by investing in a manner that differs from the conventional wisdom, when the consensus opinion appears to be wrong.

A _____ believes that certain crowd behavior among investors can lead to exploitable mispricings in securities markets. For example, widespread pessimism about a stock can drive a price so low that it overstates the company's risks, and understates its prospects for returning to profitability.

a. Day trading
b. Contrarian
c. Direct access trading
d. Secured debt

11. In statistics, a _____, is a type of finite impulse response filter used to analyze a set of data points by creating a series of averages of different subsets of the full data set. A _____ is not a single number, but it is a set of numbers, each of which is the average of the corresponding subset of a larger set of data points. A _____ may also use unequal weights for each data value in the subset to emphasize particular values in the subset.

a. Loans and interest, in Judaism
b. Voluntary Emissions Reductions
c. Gordon growth model
d. Moving average

Chapter 22. FINANCIAL ANALYSIS

12. _____ is concerned with the tasks of developing and applying quantitative or statistical methods to the study and elucidation of economic principles. _____ combines economic theory with statistics to analyze and test economic relationships. Theoretical _____ considers questions about the statistical properties of estimators and tests, while applied _____ is concerned with the application of econometric methods to assess economic theories.
   a. ABN Amro
   b. AAB
   c. A Random Walk Down Wall Street
   d. Econometrics

13. _____s are statistical models used in econometrics. An _____ specifies the statistical relationship that is believed to hold between the various economic quantities pertaining a particular economic phenomena under study. An _____ can be derived from a deterministic economic model by allowing for uncertainty or from an economic model which itself is stochastic.
   a. A Random Walk Down Wall Street
   b. ABN Amro
   c. AAB
   d. Econometric model

14. In economics, a _____ is a mechanism that allows people to easily buy and sell (trade) financial securities (such as stocks and bonds), commodities (such as precious metals or agricultural goods), and other fungible items of value at low transaction costs and at prices that reflect the efficient-market hypothesis.

   _____s have evolved significantly over several hundred years and are undergoing constant innovation to improve liquidity.

   Both general markets (where many commodities are traded) and specialized markets (where only one commodity is traded) exist.

   a. Cost of carry
   b. Secondary market
   c. Delta hedging
   d. Financial market

15. _____ is the standard framework of guidelines for financial accounting used in the United States of America. It includes the standards, conventions, and rules accountants follow in recording and summarizing transactions, and in the preparation of financial statements. _____ are now issued by the Financial Accounting Standards Board (FASB).
   a. Net income
   b. Revenue
   c. Depreciation
   d. Generally accepted accounting principles

16. In finance, the Acid-test or _____ or liquid ratio measures the ability of a company to use its near cash or quick assets to immediately extinguish or retire its current liabilities. Quick assets include those current assets that presumably can be quickly converted to cash at close to their book values.

   Generally, the acid test ratio should be 1:1 or better, however this varies widely by industry.

   a. P/E ratio
   b. Financial ratio
   c. Net assets
   d. Quick ratio

Chapter 22. FINANCIAL ANALYSIS

17. In finance, _____, also known as return on investment is the ratio of money gained or lost on an investment relative to the amount of money invested. The amount of money gained or lost may be referred to as interest, profit/loss, gain/loss, or net income/loss. The money invested may be referred to as the asset, capital, principal, or the cost basis of the investment.
   a. Doctrine of the Proper Law
   b. Stock or scrip dividends
   c. Rate of return
   d. Composiition of Creditors

18. _____ measures the rate of return on the ownership interest (shareholders' equity) of the common stock owners. _____ is viewed as one of the most important financial ratios. It measures a firm's efficiency at generating profits from every dollar of shareholders' equity (also known as net assets or assets minus liabilities.)
   a. Return on equity
   b. Return on sales
   c. Return of capital
   d. Diluted Earnings Per Share

19. _____ or interest coverage ratio is a measure of a company's ability to honor its debt payments. It may be calculated as either EBIT or EBITDA divided by the total interest payable.

$$\text{Times-Interest-Earned} = \frac{\text{EBIT or EBITDA}}{\text{Interest Charges}}$$

- Financial ratio
- Financial leverage
- EBIT
- EBITDA
- Debt service coverage ratio

Interest Charges = Traditionally 'charges' refers to interest expense found on the income statement.

_____ or Interest Coverage is a great tool when measuring a company's ability to meet its debt obligations.

   a. Net assets
   b. Cash conversion cycle
   c. Return of capital
   d. Times interest earned

20. _____ is a fee paid on borrowed assets. It is the price paid for the use of borrowed money , or, money earned by deposited funds . Assets that are sometimes lent with _____ include money, shares, consumer goods through hire purchase, major assets such as aircraft, and even entire factories in finance lease arrangements.
   a. AAB
   b. A Random Walk Down Wall Street
   c. Insolvency
   d. Interest

21. A _____ is a method of measuring a section of the stock market. Many indices are cited by news or financial services firms and are used to benchmark the performance of portfolios such as mutual funds.
   a. Trading curb
   b. Stock market index
   c. Program trading
   d. Stop order

22. In financial accounting, a _____ or statement of financial position is a summary of a person's or organization's balances. Assets, liabilities and ownership equity are listed as of a specific date, such as the end of its financial year. A _____ is often described as a snapshot of a company's financial condition.

Chapter 22. FINANCIAL ANALYSIS

a. Financial statements

c. Balance sheet

b. Statement of retained earnings

d. Statement on Auditing Standards No. 70: Service Organizations

23. In business and accounting, _____s are everything of value that is owned by a person or company. The balance sheet of a firm records the monetary value of the _____s owned by the firm. The two major _____ classes are tangible _____s and intangible _____s.
   a. Accounts payable
   c. Income
   b. Asset
   d. EBITDA

24. In business, _____ is the total assets minus total outside liabilities of an individual or a company. For a company, this is called shareholders' equity and may be referred to as book value. _____ is stated as at a particular point in time.
   a. Net worth
   c. Certified International Investment Analyst
   b. Restructuring
   d. Moneylender

25. _____, refers to consumption opportunity gained by an entity within a specified time frame, which is generally expressed in monetary terms. However, for households and individuals, '_____ is the sum of all the wages, salaries, profits, interests payments, rents and other forms of earnings received... in a given period of time.' For firms, _____ generally refers to net-profit: what remains of revenue after expenses have been subtracted.
   a. Accrual
   c. OIBDA
   b. Income
   d. Annual report

26. An _____ is a financial statement for companies that indicates how Revenue is transformed into net income The purpose of the _____ is to show managers and investors whether the company made or lost money during the period being reported.

The important thing to remember about an _____ is that it represents a period of time.

   a. A Random Walk Down Wall Street
   c. Income statement
   b. AAB
   d. ABN Amro

27. In financial accounting, a _____ or statement of cash flows is a financial statement that shows a company's flow of cash. The money coming into the business is called cash inflow, and money going out from the business is called cash outflow. The statement shows how changes in balance sheet and income accounts affect cash and cash equivalents, and breaks the analysis down to operating, investing, and financing activities.
   a. 7-Eleven
   c. 4-4-5 Calendar
   b. 529 plan
   d. Cash flow statement

Chapter 22. FINANCIAL ANALYSIS

28. _____ is the balance of the amounts of cash being received and paid by a business during a defined period of time, sometimes tied to a specific project. Measurement of _____ can be used

- to evaluate the state or performance of a business or project.
- to determine problems with liquidity. Being profitable does not necessarily mean being liquid. A company can fail because of a shortage of cash, even while profitable.
- to generate project rate of returns. The time of _____s into and out of projects are used as inputs to financial models such as internal rate of return, and net present value.
- to examine income or growth of a business when it is believed that accrual accounting concepts do not represent economic realities. Alternately, _____ can be used to 'validate' the net income generated by accrual accounting.

_____ as a generic term may be used differently depending on context, and certain _____ definitions may be adapted by analysts and users for their own uses. Common terms include operating _____ and free _____.

_____s can be classified into:

1. Operational _____s: Cash received or expended as a result of the company's core business activities.
2. Investment _____s: Cash received or expended through capital expenditure, investments or acquisitions.
3. Financing _____s: Cash received or expended as a result of financial activities, such as interests and dividends.

All three together - the net _____ - are necessary to reconcile the beginning cash balance to the ending cash balance. Loan draw downs or equity injections, that is just shifting of capital but no expenditure as such, are not considered in the net _____.

a. Shareholder value
c. Real option
b. Cash flow
d. Corporate finance

29. _____ refers to any type of investment that yields a regular (or fixed) return.

For example, if you lend money to a borrower and the borrower has to pay interest once a month, you have been issued a fixed-income security. When a company does this, it is often called a bond or corporate bank debt (although preferred stock is also sometimes considered to be _____).

a. 4-4-5 Calendar
c. Bond market
b. Fixed income
d. 529 plan

30. A _____ is the price of a single share of a no. of saleable stocks of the company. Once the stock is purchased, the owner becomes a shareholder of the company that issued the share.

a. Stock split
c. Trading curb
b. Whisper numbers
d. Share price

Chapter 22. FINANCIAL ANALYSIS

31. _____ is the trading of a corporation's stock or other securities (e.g. bonds or stock options) by individuals with potential access to non-public information about the company. In most countries, trading by corporate insiders such as officers, key employees, directors, and large shareholders may be legal, if this trading is done in a way that does not take advantage of non-public information. However, the term is frequently used to refer to a practice in which an insider or a related party trades based on material non-public information obtained during the performance of the insider's duties at the corporation, or otherwise in breach of a fiduciary duty or other relationship of trust and confidence or where the non-public information was misappropriated from the company.

a. Equity investment
b. Insider trading
c. Intellidex
d. Open outcry

32. The phrase _____ refers to the aspect of corporate strategy, corporate finance and management dealing with the buying, selling and combining of different companies that can aid, finance, or help a growing company in a given industry grow rapidly without having to create another business entity.

An acquisition, also known as a takeover, is the buying of one company (the 'target') by another. An acquisition may be friendly or hostile.

a. 4-4-5 Calendar
b. 7-Eleven
c. 529 plan
d. Mergers and acquisitions

33. In economics and contract theory, _____ deals with the study of decisions in transactions where one party has more or better information than the other. This creates an imbalance of power in transactions which can sometimes cause the transactions to go awry. Examples of this problem are adverse selection and moral hazard.

a. A Random Walk Down Wall Street
b. AAB
c. ABN Amro
d. Information asymmetry

34. In finance, a _____ is a debt security, in which the authorized issuer owes the holders a debt and, depending on the terms of the _____, is obliged to pay interest (the coupon) and/or to repay the principal at a later date, termed maturity.

Thus a _____ is a loan: the issuer is the borrower, the _____ holder is the lender, and the coupon is the interest. _____s provide the borrower with external funds to finance long-term investments, or, in the case of government _____s, to finance current expenditure.

a. Catastrophe bonds
b. Puttable bond
c. Convertible bond
d. Bond

35. In finance, a _____ is a type of bond that can be converted into shares of stock in the issuing company, usually at some pre-announced ratio. It is a hybrid security with debt- and equity-like features. Although it typically has a low coupon rate, the holder is compensated with the ability to convert the bond to common stock, usually at a substantial discount to the stock's market value.

a. Gilts
b. Corporate bond
c. Bond fund
d. Convertible bond

Chapter 22. FINANCIAL ANALYSIS

36. An _____ is a contract written by a seller that conveys to the buyer the right -- but not the obligation -- to buy (in the case of a call _____) or to sell (in the case of a put _____) a particular asset, such as a piece of property such as, among others, a futures contract. In return for granting the _____, the seller collects a payment (the premium) from the buyer.

For example, buying a call _____ provides the right to buy a specified quantity of a security at a set strike price at some time on or before expiration, while buying a put _____ provides the right to sell.

    a. Option
    c. AT'T Mobility LLC
    b. Amortization
    d. Annuity

37. In financial accounting, the term _____ is most commonly used to describe any part of shareholders' equity, except for basic share capital. Sometimes, the term is used instead of the term provision; such a use, however, is inconsistent with the terminology suggested by International Accounting Standards Board. For more information about provisions, see provision (accounting.)

    a. Closing entries
    c. FIFO and LIFO accounting
    b. Treasury stock
    d. Reserve

Chapter 23. INVESTMENT MANAGEMENT

1. An _____ is any government regulation or law that encourages or discourages foreign investment in the local economy, e.g. currency exchange limits.

As globalization integrates the economies of neighboring and of trading states, they are typically forced to trade off such rules as part of a common tax, tariff and trade regime, e.g. as defined by a free trade pact. _____ favoring local investors over global ones is typically discouraged in such pacts, and the idea of a separate _____ rapidly becomes a fiction or fantasy, as real decisions reflect the real need for nations to compete for investment, even from their own local investors.

 a. AAB
 b. A Random Walk Down Wall Street
 c. ABN Amro
 d. Investment policy

2. The _____ is the guaranteed payoff at which a person is 'indifferent' between accepting the guaranteed payoff and a higher but uncertain payoff. (It is the amount of the higher payout minus the risk premium).
 a. 529 plan
 b. 4-4-5 Calendar
 c. 7-Eleven
 d. Certainty equivalent

3. _____ refers to a portfolio management strategy where the manager makes specific investments with the goal of outperforming an investment benchmark index. Investors or mutual funds that do not aspire to create a return in excess of a benchmark index will often invest in an index fund that replicates as closely as possible the investment weighting and returns of that index; this is called passive management. _____ is the opposite of passive management, because in passive management the manager does not seek to outperform the benchmark index.
 a. A Random Walk Down Wall Street
 b. ABN Amro
 c. AAB
 d. Active management

4. _____ is a financial strategy in which a fund manager makes as few portfolio decisions as possible, in order to minimize transaction costs, including the incidence of capital gains tax. One popular method is to mimic the performance of an externally specified index--called 'index funds'. The ethos of an index fund is aptly summed up in the injunction to an index fund manager: 'Don't just do something, sit there!'

_____ is most common on the equity market, where index funds track a stock market index, but it is becoming more common in other investment types, including bonds, commodities and hedge funds.

 a. Net asset value
 b. Savings and loan association
 c. Trust company
 d. Passive management

5. A _____ is a fungible, negotiable instrument representing financial value. They are broadly categorized into debt securities (such as banknotes, bonds and debentures), and equity securities; e.g., common stocks. The company or other entity issuing the _____ is called the issuer.
 a. Security
 b. Book entry
 c. Securities lending
 d. Tracking stock

Chapter 23. INVESTMENT MANAGEMENT

6. _____, authored by professors Benjamin Graham and David Dodd of Columbia Business School, laid the intellectual foundation for what would later be called value investing. The work was first published in 1934, following unprecedented losses on Wall Street. In summing up lessons learned, Graham and Dodd chided Wall Street for its myopic focus on a company's reported earnings per share, and were particularly harsh on the favored 'earnings trends.' They encouraged investors to take an entirely different approach by gauging the rough value of the operating business that lay behind the security.

a. Growth stocks
b. 4-4-5 Calendar
c. Stock valuation
d. Security analysis

7. In business and accounting, _____s are everything of value that is owned by a person or company. The balance sheet of a firm records the monetary value of the _____s owned by the firm. The two major _____ classes are tangible _____s and intangible _____s.

a. Income
b. EBITDA
c. Accounts payable
d. Asset

8. _____ is a term used to refer to how an investor distributes his or her investments among various classes of investment vehicles (e.g., stocks and bonds.)

A large part of financial planning is finding an _____ that is appropriate for a given person in terms of their appetite for and ability to shoulder risk. This can depend on various factors; see investor profile.

a. Alternative investment
b. Investing online
c. Investment performance
d. Asset allocation

9. _____ is a method of investing in which investors modify their asset allocation according to the valuation of the markets in which they are invested. Thus, someone invested heavily in stocks might reduce his position when he perceives that other securities, such as bonds, are poised to outperform stocks. Unlike stock picking, in which the investor predicts which individual stocks will perform well, _____ involves only judgments of the future return of complete markets or sectors.

a. Security market line
b. Market timing
c. Divestment
d. Tactical asset allocation

10. _____ refers to different style characteristics of equities, bonds or financial derivatives within a given investment philosophy.

Theory would favor a combination of big capitalization, passive and value. Of course one could almost get that when investing in an important Index like S'P 500, Euro-Stoxx or the like.

a. ABN Amro
b. AAB
c. A Random Walk Down Wall Street
d. Investment style

11. _____ is the strategy of making buy or sell decisions of financial assets (often stocks) by attempting to predict future market price movements. The prediction may be based on an outlook of market or economic conditions resulting from technical or fundamental analysis. This is an investment strategy based on the outlook for an aggregate market, rather than for a particular financial asset.

Chapter 23. INVESTMENT MANAGEMENT

a. Late trading
b. Market timing
c. Portable alpha
d. Divestment

12. _____ is a distortion of evidence or data that arises from the way that the data are collected. It is sometimes referred to as the selection effect. The term _____ most often refers to the distortion of a statistical analysis, due to the method of collecting samples.
   a. Selection bias
   b. 529 plan
   c. 4-4-5 Calendar
   d. 7-Eleven

13. _____ is a term that refers both to:

   - a formal discipline used to help appraise, or assess, the case for a project or proposal, which itself is a process known as project appraisal; and
   - an informal approach to making decisions of any kind.

Under both definitions the process involves, whether explicitly or implicitly, weighing the total expected costs against the total expected benefits of one or more actions in order to choose the best or most profitable option.

A hallmark of _____ is that all benefits and all costs are expressed in money terms, and are adjusted for the time value of money, so that all flows of benefits and flows of project costs over time (which tend to occur at different points in time) are expressed on a common basis in terms of their present value.

   a. Cost-benefit analysis
   b. 7-Eleven
   c. 4-4-5 Calendar
   d. 529 plan

14. An _____ is a swap where a set of future cash flows are exchanged between two counterparties. The two cash flows are usually referred to as 'legs'. One of these cash flow streams can be pegged to floating rate of interest or pay a fixed rate
   a. Interest rate swap
   b. Interest rate derivative
   c. Interest rate future
   d. Equity swap

15. In finance, a _____ is a derivative in which two counterparties agree to exchange one stream of cash flows against another stream. These streams are called the legs of the _____.

The cash flows are calculated over a notional principal amount, which is usually not exchanged between counterparties.

   a. Volatility arbitrage
   b. Volatility swap
   c. Local volatility
   d. Swap

16. _____ is a fee paid on borrowed assets. It is the price paid for the use of borrowed money, or, money earned by deposited funds. Assets that are sometimes lent with _____ include money, shares, consumer goods through hire purchase, major assets such as aircraft, and even entire factories in finance lease arrangements.
   a. Insolvency
   b. Interest
   c. A Random Walk Down Wall Street
   d. AAB

Chapter 23. INVESTMENT MANAGEMENT

17. An _____ is the price a borrower pays for the use of money they do not own, and the return a lender receives for deferring the use of funds, by lending it to the borrower. _____s are normally expressed as a percentage rate over the period of one year.

_____s targets are also a vital tool of monetary policy and are used to control variables like investment, inflation, and unemployment.

    a. A Random Walk Down Wall Street   b. AAB
    c. ABN Amro   d. Interest rate

18. An _____ is a derivative in which one party exchanges a stream of interest payments for another party's stream of cash flows. _____s can be used by hedgers to manage their fixed or floating assets and liabilities. They can also be used by speculators to replicate unfunded bond exposures to profit from changes in interest rates.

    a. Equity swap   b. International Swaps and Derivatives Association
    c. Interest rate Swap   d. Implied volatility

19. A _____ or stock divide increases or decreases the number of shares in a public company. The price is adjusted such that the before and after market capitalization of the company remains the same and dilution does not occur. Options and warrants are included.

    a. Contract for difference   b. Stop price
    c. Stop order   d. Stock split

20. _____ or financing is to provide capital (funds), which means money for a project, a person, a business or any other private or public institutions.

Those funds can be allocated for either short term or long term purposes. The health fund is a new way of _____ private healthcare centers.

    a. Proxy fight   b. Synthetic CDO
    c. Product life cycle   d. Funding

Chapter 24. PORTFOLIO PERFORMANCE EVALUATION

1. The _____ is one of several stock market indices, created by nineteenth-century Wall Street Journal editor and Dow Jones ' Company co-founder Charles Dow. Dow compiled the index to gauge the performance of the industrial sector of the American stock market. It is the second-oldest U.S. market index, after the Dow Jones Transportation Average, which Dow also created.

   a. 4-4-5 Calendar
   b. 7-Eleven
   c. 529 plan
   d. Dow Jones Industrial Average

2. In descriptive statistics, a _____ or boxplot is a convenient way of graphically depicting groups of numerical data through their five-number summaries, lower quartile, median, upper quartile, and largest observation A boxplot may also indicate which observations, if any, might be considered outliers.

   Boxplots can be useful to display differences between populations without making any assumptions of the underlying statistical distribution: they are non-parametric.

   a. Box plot
   b. 4-4-5 Calendar
   c. 7-Eleven
   d. 529 plan

3. In economics and finance, _____ is the practice of taking advantage of a price differential between two or more markets: striking a combination of matching deals that capitalize upon the imbalance, the profit being the difference between the market prices. When used by academics, an _____ is a transaction that involves no negative cash flow at any probabilistic or temporal state and a positive cash flow in at least one state; in simple terms, a risk-free profit.

   a. Issuer
   b. Initial margin
   c. Efficient-market hypothesis
   d. Arbitrage

4. In finance, a _____ is a debt security, in which the authorized issuer owes the holders a debt and, depending on the terms of the _____, is obliged to pay interest (the coupon) and/or to repay the principal at a later date, termed maturity.

   Thus a _____ is a loan: the issuer is the borrower, the _____ holder is the lender, and the coupon is the interest. _____s provide the borrower with external funds to finance long-term investments, or, in the case of government _____s, to finance current expenditure.

   a. Bond
   b. Catastrophe bonds
   c. Convertible bond
   d. Puttable bond

5. The _____ is a financial market where participants buy and sell debt securities, usually in the form of bonds. As of 2006, the size of the international _____ is an estimated $45 trillion, of which the size of the outstanding U.S. _____ debt was $25.2 trillion.

   Nearly all of the $923 billion average daily trading volume in the U.S. _____ takes place between broker-dealers and large institutions in a decentralized, over-the-counter market.

   a. Bond market
   b. Fixed income
   c. 529 plan
   d. 4-4-5 Calendar

6. In the United States, the Financial Industry Regulatory Authority (FINRA) is a self-regulatory organization (SRO) under the Securities Exchange Act of 1934, successor to the _____, Inc.

Chapter 24. PORTFOLIO PERFORMANCE EVALUATION

FINRA is responsible for regulatory oversight of all securities firms that do business with the public; professional training, testing and licensing of registered persons; arbitration and mediation; market regulation by contract for The NASDAQ Stock Market, Inc., the American Stock Exchange LLC, and the International Securities Exchange, LLC; and industry utilities, such as Trade Reporting Facilities and other over-the-counter operations.

a. 7-Eleven
c. 4-4-5 Calendar
b. 529 plan
d. National Association of Securities Dealers

7. The _____ is a stock exchange based in New York City, New York. It is the largest stock exchange in the world by dollar value of its listed companies securities. As of October 2008, the combined capitalization of all domestic _____ listed companies was $10.1 trillion.

a. 7-Eleven
c. 4-4-5 Calendar
b. 529 plan
d. New York Stock Exchange

8. A _____ is a fungible, negotiable instrument representing financial value. They are broadly categorized into debt securities (such as banknotes, bonds and debentures), and equity securities; e.g., common stocks. The company or other entity issuing the _____ is called the issuer.

a. Securities lending
c. Book entry
b. Security
d. Tracking stock

9. _____ is a mathematical science pertaining to the collection, analysis, interpretation or explanation, and presentation of data. It also provides tools for prediction and forecasting based on data. It is applicable to a wide variety of academic disciplines, from the natural and social sciences to the humanities, government and business.

a. Statistics
c. Sample size
b. Mean
d. Covariance

10. A _____, securities exchange or (in Europe) bourse is a corporation or mutual organization which provides 'trading' facilities for stock brokers and traders, to trade stocks and other securities. _____s also provide facilities for the issue and redemption of securities as well as other financial instruments and capital events including the payment of income and dividends. The securities traded on a _____ include: shares issued by companies, unit trusts and other pooled investment products and bonds.

a. Stock Exchange
c. 529 plan
b. 4-4-5 Calendar
d. 7-Eleven

11. A _____ is a method of measuring a section of the stock market. Many indices are cited by news or financial services firms and are used to benchmark the performance of portfolios such as mutual funds.

a. Stop order
c. Trading curb
b. Program trading
d. Stock market index

12. The _____, in mathematics, is a type of mean or average, which indicates the central tendency or typical value of a set of numbers. It is similar to the arithmetic mean, which is what most people think of with the word 'average,' except that instead of adding the set of numbers and then dividing the sum by the count of numbers in the set, n, the numbers are multiplied and then the nth root of the resulting product is taken.

Chapter 24. PORTFOLIO PERFORMANCE EVALUATION

For instance, the _____ of two numbers, say 2 and 8, is just the square root (i.e., the second root) of their product, 16, which is 4.

a. Geometric mean
c. Statistics
b. Kurtosis
d. Standard deviation

13. The _____ is composed of all of the companies that are included in the Value Line Investment Survey.

There are currently 1,626 companies included in the index that are publicly listed on the following exchanges:

- American Stock Exchange - 8 companies
- NASDAQ - 511 companies
- New York Stock Exchange - 1,087 companies
- Toronto Stock Exchange - 20 companies

The _____ has been traded on the futures market at the Kansas City Board of Trade since 1982.

The original index was released on June 30, 1961 and was an equally weighted index using a geometric average. Because it is based on a geometric average the daily change is closest to the median stock price change.

a. 4-4-5 Calendar
c. 529 plan
b. 7-Eleven
d. Value Line Composite Index

14. In statistics, _____ has two related meanings:

- the arithmetic _____
- the expected value of a random variable, which is also called the population _____.

It is sometimes stated that the '_____' is average. This is incorrect if '_____' is taken in the specific sense of 'arithmetic _____' as there are different types of averages: the _____, median, and mode. Other simple statistical analyses use measures of spread, such as range, interquartile range, or standard deviation. For a real-valued random variable X, the _____ is the expectation of X. Note that not every probability distribution has a defined _____; see the Cauchy distribution for an example.

a. Sample size
c. Harmonic mean
b. Probability distribution
d. Mean

15. _____ is a risk-adjusted measure of the so-called active return on an investment. It is the return in excess of the compensation for the risk borne, and thus commonly used to assess active managers' performances. Often, the return of a benchmark is subtracted in order to consider relative performance, which yields Jensen's _____.
a. Option
c. Annuity
b. Amortization
d. Alpha

16. A _____ is a linear regression in which there is only one covariate (predictor variable.)

Chapter 24. PORTFOLIO PERFORMANCE EVALUATION

_____ is used to evaluate the linear relationship between two variables. One example could be the relationship between muscle strength and lean body mass.

a. 529 plan
c. 4-4-5 Calendar
b. Simple linear regression
d. 7-Eleven

17. In statistics, _____ is used for two things;

- to construct a simple formula that will predict a value or values for a variable given the value of another variable.
- to test whether and how a given variable is related to another variable or variables.

_____ is a form of regression analysis in which the relationship between one or more independent variables and another variable, called the dependent variable, is modelled by a least squares function, called a _____ equation. This function is a linear combination of one or more model parameters, called regression coefficients. A _____ equation with one independent variable represents a straight line when the predicted value (i.e. the dependant variable from the regression equation) is plotted against the independent variable: this is called a simple _____. However, note that 'linear' does not refer to this straight line, but rather to the way in which the regression coefficients occur in the regression equation.

a. Stock trader
c. Foreign Language and Area Studies
b. Linear Regression
d. Wall Street Crash of 1929

18. _____ is a graph created by investors to measure the risk of risky and risk-free assets. The graph displays to the investors on the return they can make by taking on a certain level of risk. It is also known as a 'reward-to-variability ratio'.

a. Divestment
c. Dollar cost averaging
b. Portfolio investment
d. Capital allocation line

19. The _____ is a measure of the excess return (or Risk Premium) per unit of risk in an investment asset or a trading strategy it is defined as:

$$S = \frac{R - R_f}{\sigma} = \frac{E[R - R_f]}{\sqrt{\mathrm{var}[R - R_f]}},$$

where R is the asset return, R_f is the return on a benchmark asset, such as the risk free rate of return, $E[R - R_f]$ is the expected value of the excess of the asset return over the benchmark return, and σ is the standard deviation of the asset excess return.

Note, if R_f is a constant risk free return throughout the period,

$$\sqrt{\mathrm{var}[R - R_f]} = \sqrt{\mathrm{var}[R]}.$$

Chapter 24. PORTFOLIO PERFORMANCE EVALUATION

The _____ is used to characterize how well the return of an asset compensates the investor for the risk taken. When comparing two assets each with the expected return E[R] against the same benchmark with return R_f, the asset with the higher _____ gives more return for the same risk.

a. P/E ratio
c. Current ratio
b. Receivables turnover ratio
d. Sharpe ratio

20. _____ is the strategy of making buy or sell decisions of financial assets (often stocks) by attempting to predict future market price movements. The prediction may be based on an outlook of market or economic conditions resulting from technical or fundamental analysis. This is an investment strategy based on the outlook for an aggregate market, rather than for a particular financial asset.

a. Divestment
c. Late trading
b. Portable alpha
d. Market timing

21. A _____ is a portfolio consisting of a weighted sum of every asset in the market, with weights in the proportions that they exist in the market (with the necessary assumption that these assets are infinitely divisible.)

Neha Tyagi's critique (1977) states that this is only a theoretical concept, as to create a _____ for investment purposes in practice would necessarily include every single possible available asset, including real estate, precious metals, stamp collections, jewelry, and anything with any worth, as the theoretical market being referred to would be the world market. As a result, proxies for the market are used in practice by investors.

a. Market portfolio
c. Market price
b. Delta neutral
d. Central Securities Depository

22. In finance, the _____ is used to determine a theoretically appropriate required rate of return of an asset, if that asset is to be added to an already well-diversified portfolio, given that asset's non-diversifiable risk. The model takes into account the asset's sensitivity to non-diversifiable risk (also known as systemic risk or market risk), often represented by the quantity beta (β) in the financial industry, as well as the expected return of the market and the expected return of a theoretical risk-free asset.

The model was introduced by Jack Treynor (1961, 1962), William Sharpe (1964), John Lintner (1965a,b) and Jan Mossin (1966) independently, building on the earlier work of Harry Markowitz on diversification and modern portfolio theory.

a. Cox-Ingersoll-Ross model
c. Hull-White model
b. Capital asset pricing model
d. Random walk hypothesis

23. _____ or Investment _____ is a set of techniques that performance analysts use to explain why a portfolio's performance differed from the benchmark. This difference between the portfolio return and the benchmark return is known as the active return. The active return is the component of a portfolio's performance that arises from the fact that the portfolio is actively managed.

Chapter 24. PORTFOLIO PERFORMANCE EVALUATION

a. Central Securities Depository
b. Performance attribution
c. Convertible arbitrage
d. Delta neutral

24. _____ or net present worth (NPW) is defined as the total present value (PV) of a time series of cash flows. It is a standard method for using the time value of money to appraise long-term projects. Used for capital budgeting, and widely throughout economics, it measures the excess or shortfall of cash flows, in present value terms, once financing charges are met.

a. Negative gearing
b. Net present value
c. Tax shield
d. Present value of costs

25. A _____ is a person who makes investment decisions using money other people have placed under his or her control. In other words, it is a financial career involved in investment management. They work with a team of analysts and researchers, and are ultimately responsible for establishing an investment strategy, selecting appropriate investments and allocating each investment properly for a fund- or asset-management vehicle.

a. Portfolio manager
b. Day trader
c. Purchasing manager
d. Financial analyst

26. _____ is the value on a given date of a future payment or series of future payments, discounted to reflect the time value of money and other factors such as investment risk. _____ calculations are widely used in business and economics to provide a means to compare cash flows at different times on a meaningful 'like to like' basis.

The most commonly applied model of the time value of money is compound interest.

a. Present value of benefits
b. Net present value
c. Present value
d. Negative gearing

27. _____ are government bonds issued by the United States Department of the Treasury through the Bureau of the Public Debt. They are the debt financing instruments of the U.S. Federal government, and they are often referred to simply as Treasuries or Treasurys. There are four types of marketable _____: Treasury bills, Treasury notes, Treasury bonds, and Treasury Inflation Protected Securities (TIPS.)

a. Treasury Inflation Protected Securities
b. Treasury securities
c. 4-4-5 Calendar
d. Treasury Inflation-Protected Securities

Chapter 25. INTERNATIONAL INVESTING

1. The _____ is the market for securities, where companies and governments can raise longterm funds. The _____ includes the stock market and the bond market. Financial regulators, such as the U.S. Securities and Exchange Commission, oversee the _____s in their designated countries to ensure that investors are protected against fraud.
   a. Forward market
   b. Spot rate
   c. Delta neutral
   d. Capital market

2. A _____ is a portfolio consisting of a weighted sum of every asset in the market, with weights in the proportions that they exist in the market (with the necessary assumption that these assets are infinitely divisible.)

   Neha Tyagi's critique (1977) states that this is only a theoretical concept, as to create a _____ for investment purposes in practice would necessarily include every single possible available asset, including real estate, precious metals, stamp collections, jewelry, and anything with any worth, as the theoretical market being referred to would be the world market. As a result, proxies for the market are used in practice by investors.

   a. Market price
   b. Central Securities Depository
   c. Market portfolio
   d. Delta neutral

3. A _____, securities exchange or (in Europe) bourse is a corporation or mutual organization which provides 'trading' facilities for stock brokers and traders, to trade stocks and other securities. _____s also provide facilities for the issue and redemption of securities as well as other financial instruments and capital events including the payment of income and dividends. The securities traded on a _____ include: shares issued by companies, unit trusts and other pooled investment products and bonds.
   a. Stock Exchange
   b. 529 plan
   c. 4-4-5 Calendar
   d. 7-Eleven

4. The term _____ is used to describe a nation's social, or business activity in the process of rapid industrialization. _____ are generally less-wealthy than the developed world, and are wealthier (or the wealthiest of) the developing world. According to The Economist many people find the term dated, but a new term has yet to gain much traction.
   a. ABN Amro
   b. AAB
   c. A Random Walk Down Wall Street
   d. Emerging markets

5. _____ is a type of risk faced by investors, corporations, and governments. It is a risk that can be understood and managed with proper aforethought and investment.

   Broadly, _____ refers to the complications businesses and governments may face as a result of what are commonly referred to as political decisions--or 'any political change that alters the expected outcome and value of a given economic action by changing the probability of achieving business objectives.' .

   a. Capital asset
   b. Mid price
   c. Single-index model
   d. Political Risk

Chapter 25. INTERNATIONAL INVESTING

6. _____ is a form of risk that arises from the change in price of one currency against another. Whenever investors or companies have assets or business operations across national borders, they face _____ if their positions are not hedged.

- Transaction risk is the risk that exchange rates will change unfavourably over time. It can be hedged against using forward currency contracts;
- Translation risk is an accounting risk, proportional to the amount of assets held in foreign currencies. Changes in the exchange rate over time will render a report inaccurate, and so assets are usually balanced by borrowings in that currency.

The exchange risk associated with a foreign denominated instrument is a key element in foreign investment. This risk flows from differential monetary policy and growth in real productivity, which results in differential inflation rates.

a. Tracking error
b. Credit risk
c. Market risk
d. Currency risk

7. The _____ is the weighted-average most likely outcome in gambling, probability theory, economics or finance.

In gambling and probability theory, there is usually a discrete set of possible outcomes. In this case, _____ is a measure of the relative balance of win or loss weighted by their chances of occurring.

a. ABN Amro
b. AAB
c. A Random Walk Down Wall Street
d. Expected return

8. An _____ represents the ownership in the shares of a foreign company trading on US financial markets. The stock of many non-US companies trades on US exchanges through the use of _____s. _____s enable US investors to buy shares in foreign companies without undertaking cross-border transactions.

a. AAB
b. ABN Amro
c. A Random Walk Down Wall Street
d. American Depository Receipt

9. In the United States, the Financial Industry Regulatory Authority (FINRA) is a self-regulatory organization (SRO) under the Securities Exchange Act of 1934, successor to the _____, Inc.

FINRA is responsible for regulatory oversight of all securities firms that do business with the public; professional training, testing and licensing of registered persons; arbitration and mediation; market regulation by contract for The NASDAQ Stock Market, Inc., the American Stock Exchange LLC, and the International Securities Exchange, LLC; and industry utilities, such as Trade Reporting Facilities and other over-the-counter operations.

a. 4-4-5 Calendar
b. 529 plan
c. 7-Eleven
d. National Association of Securities Dealers

10. The _____ is a stock exchange based in New York City, New York. It is the largest stock exchange in the world by dollar value of its listed companies securities. As of October 2008, the combined capitalization of all domestic _____ listed companies was $10.1 trillion.

Chapter 25. INTERNATIONAL INVESTING

a. New York Stock Exchange
b. 529 plan
c. 7-Eleven
d. 4-4-5 Calendar

11. A _____ is a fungible, negotiable instrument representing financial value. They are broadly categorized into debt securities (such as banknotes, bonds and debentures), and equity securities; e.g., common stocks. The company or other entity issuing the _____ is called the issuer.

a. Tracking stock
b. Book entry
c. Security
d. Securities lending

12. In probability theory and statistics, _____ indicates the strength and direction of a linear relationship between two random variables. That is in contrast with the usage of the term in colloquial speech, which denotes any relationship, not necessarily linear. In general statistical usage, _____ or co-relation refers to the departure of two random variables from independence.

a. Probability distribution
b. Geometric mean
c. Correlation
d. Variance

13. In business and accounting, _____s are everything of value that is owned by a person or company. The balance sheet of a firm records the monetary value of the _____s owned by the firm. The two major _____ classes are tangible _____s and intangible _____s.

a. Income
b. Accounts payable
c. EBITDA
d. Asset

14. The _____ is a U.S. government-owned corporation within the Department of Housing and Urban Development

Ginnie Mae provides guarantees on mortgage-backed securities backed by federally insured or guaranteed loans, mainly loans issued by the Federal Housing Administration, Department of Veterans Affairs, Rural Housing Service, and Office of Public and Indian Housing. Ginnie Mae securities are the only MBS that are guaranteed by the United States government.

a. Case-Shiller Home Price Indices
b. GNMA
c. Cash budget
d. Certified Emission Reductions

15. The _____ is a U.S. government-owned corporation within the Department of Housing and Urban Development

Ginnie Mae provides guarantees on mortgage-backed securities backed by federally insured or guaranteed loans, mainly loans issued by the Federal Housing Administration, Department of Veterans Affairs, Rural Housing Service, and Office of Public and Indian Housing. Ginnie Mae securities are the only MBS that are guaranteed by the United States government.

a. Graduated payment mortgage
b. 4-4-5 Calendar
c. Jumbo mortgage
d. Government National Mortgage Association

16. An _____ is an investment product other than traditional investments such as stocks, bonds or cash.

This broad definition makes it impossible to list all alternative strategies, but the most important areas are real estate, private equity, venture capital,commodities, and hedged or absolute return strategies. Wine, art and antiques, indeed any business of value, might also be considered as an _____.

a. Asset allocation
c. Investing online
b. Investment decisions
d. Alternative investment

17. In finance, _____ (or gearing) is borrowing money to supplement existing funds for investment in such a way that the potential positive or negative outcome is magnified and/or enhanced. It generally refers to using borrowed funds, or debt, so as to attempt to increase the returns to equity. Deleveraging is the action of reducing borrowings.

a. Financial endowment
c. Leverage
b. Pension fund
d. Limited partnership

18. _____ is a type of private equity capital typically provided to early-stage, high-potential, growth companies in the interest of generating a return through an eventual realization event such as an IPO or trade sale of the company. _____ investments are generally made as cash in exchange for shares in the invested company. It is typical for _____ investors to identify and back companies in high technology industries such as biotechnology and ICT.

a. Tail risk
c. Treasury Inflation-Protected Securities
b. Venture capital
d. Probability distribution

ANSWER KEY

Chapter 1

1. c	2. c	3. d	4. a	5. c	6. c	7. d	8. a	9. d	10. d
11. d	12. a	13. b	14. b	15. b	16. c	17. d	18. d	19. c	20. c
21. a	22. d	23. d	24. b	25. d	26. b	27. b	28. d	29. c	30. a
31. a	32. b	33. c	34. b	35. a	36. d	37. b	38. b	39. d	40. d
41. d	42. b	43. c	44. d	45. a	46. a	47. d	48. c	49. d	50. d

Chapter 2

1. d	2. c	3. d	4. b	5. d	6. d	7. d	8. a	9. d	10. a
11. b	12. a	13. d	14. c	15. b	16. c	17. a	18. b	19. d	20. d
21. d	22. d	23. c	24. b	25. d	26. d	27. d	28. a	29. b	30. d
31. d	32. d	33. a	34. d	35. d					

Chapter 3

1. d	2. c	3. a	4. a	5. a	6. c	7. b	8. d	9. d	10. d
11. a	12. d	13. b	14. d	15. d	16. d	17. d	18. b	19. d	20. b
21. d	22. d	23. d	24. c	25. d	26. d	27. d	28. b	29. c	30. d
31. d	32. d	33. d	34. b	35. b	36. a	37. d	38. d	39. d	40. c
41. d	42. d	43. d	44. d	45. d	46. a	47. b			

Chapter 4

1. b	2. d	3. a	4. d	5. c	6. d	7. b	8. b	9. b

Chapter 5

1. a	2. b	3. d	4. b	5. d	6. b	7. a	8. b	9. b	10. b
11. a	12. d	13. d	14. d	15. b	16. b	17. d	18. d	19. a	20. d
21. b	22. c	23. a	24. d	25. c	26. d	27. b	28. a	29. d	30. d
31. a	32. d								

Chapter 6

1. b	2. d	3. c	4. d	5. d	6. b	7. c	8. d	9. d	10. a
11. c	12. a	13. c	14. a	15. d	16. d	17. d	18. b	19. d	

Chapter 7

1. c	2. b	3. b	4. a	5. d	6. d	7. a	8. d	9. d	10. c

Chapter 8

1. d	2. d	3. a	4. a	5. d	6. b	7. d

Chapter 9

1. d	2. a	3. a	4. d	5. b	6. b	7. d	8. d	9. b	10. b
11. d	12. d	13. d	14. b	15. b	16. d	17. b	18. a	19. b	20. b
21. a	22. a	23. b	24. c	25. d	26. b	27. a	28. d	29. d	

Chapter 10

1. d	2. a	3. d	4. b	5. d	6. d	7. d

Chapter 11
    1. c   2. a   3. c   4. b

Chapter 12
1. b	2. a	3. c	4. d	5. d	6. d	7. d	8. a	9. d	10. d
11. c	12. d	13. b	14. d	15. d	16. d	17. a	18. b	19. b	20. a
21. d	22. b	23. b	24. d	25. c	26. d	27. d	28. a	29. c	30. c
31. b	32. d	33. c	34. d						

Chapter 13
1. d	2. b	3. b	4. d	5. d	6. d	7. b	8. d	9. d	10. b
11. d	12. a	13. d	14. d	15. d	16. d	17. d	18. c	19. c	20. d
21. d	22. a	23. d	24. b	25. d	26. c	27. d	28. d	29. d	30. c
31. b	32. d	33. a	34. c	35. a	36. c	37. d	38. c	39. a	40. d
41. b	42. a	43. d	44. d	45. d	46. d	47. c	48. d	49. a	50. c
51. d	52. c	53. b	54. d	55. c	56. d	57. a	58. b	59. a	60. a
61. d	62. b	63. c	64. d	65. d	66. d	67. c			

Chapter 14
1. a	2. c	3. d	4. d	5. b	6. a	7. b	8. c	9. a	10. a
11. c	12. a	13. d	14. c	15. b	16. d	17. c	18. d	19. d	20. b
21. a	22. d	23. c	24. d	25. d	26. a	27. a	28. d	29. c	30. a
31. a	32. b	33. a	34. a	35. d	36. d	37. a	38. d		

Chapter 15
1. c	2. d	3. d	4. a	5. d	6. d	7. d	8. a	9. a	10. c
11. a	12. b	13. b	14. d	15. d	16. d	17. a	18. d	19. a	20. b
21. c	22. d	23. d	24. d	25. d	26. d	27. b	28. a	29. d	30. b
31. d	32. d	33. b	34. d	35. a	36. b	37. d			

Chapter 16
1. a	2. b	3. d	4. d	5. d	6. c	7. c	8. d	9. a	10. b
11. c	12. a	13. b	14. c	15. c	16. d	17. d	18. d	19. d	20. b
21. b	22. d	23. b	24. a	25. d	26. d	27. c	28. c	29. d	30. c
31. b	32. d	33. a	34. c	35. a	36. d	37. a	38. a	39. d	40. d
41. d	42. d	43. d	44. d	45. b	46. c	47. d	48. d	49. d	50. d
51. a	52. b	53. b	54. d	55. d	56. d	57. d	58. d	59. d	60. c
61. b	62. b	63. b	64. d	65. d	66. c				

Chapter 17
1. b	2. d	3. d	4. d	5. d	6. a	7. c	8. d	9. d	10. d
11. d	12. d	13. d	14. a	15. d	16. b	17. d	18. a	19. d	20. d
21. a	22. d								

ANSWER KEY

Chapter 18
1. d	2. d	3. d	4. c	5. a	6. d	7. a	8. a	9. b	10. d
11. b	12. d	13. d	14. c	15. d	16. a	17. c	18. d	19. b	20. a

Chapter 19
1. c	2. d	3. b	4. b	5. d	6. b	7. b	8. c	9. d	10. b
11. c	12. d	13. c	14. d	15. b	16. c	17. d	18. c	19. b	20. d
21. d	22. d	23. b	24. d	25. b	26. d	27. b	28. b	29. c	30. d
31. d	32. a	33. c	34. c	35. b	36. c	37. d	38. b	39. b	40. d
41. c	42. b	43. d							

Chapter 20
1. a	2. b	3. d	4. a	5. c	6. d	7. d	8. d	9. b	10. d
11. b	12. d	13. d	14. d	15. d	16. d	17. b	18. d	19. d	20. d
21. c	22. b	23. d	24. d	25. c	26. d	27. d	28. d	29. d	30. d
31. a	32. b	33. d	34. d	35. d	36. a	37. c	38. d	39. b	40. b
41. a									

Chapter 21
1. b	2. d	3. d	4. b	5. d	6. c	7. d	8. b	9. b	10. a
11. a	12. d	13. d	14. b	15. d	16. b	17. d	18. a	19. c	20. d
21. a	22. b	23. a	24. a	25. d					

Chapter 22
1. a	2. c	3. d	4. a	5. d	6. b	7. d	8. d	9. a	10. b
11. d	12. d	13. d	14. d	15. d	16. d	17. c	18. a	19. d	20. d
21. b	22. c	23. b	24. a	25. b	26. c	27. d	28. b	29. b	30. d
31. b	32. d	33. d	34. d	35. d	36. a	37. d			

Chapter 23
1. d	2. d	3. d	4. d	5. a	6. d	7. d	8. d	9. d	10. d
11. b	12. a	13. a	14. d	15. d	16. b	17. d	18. c	19. d	20. d

Chapter 24
1. d	2. a	3. d	4. a	5. a	6. d	7. d	8. b	9. a	10. a
11. d	12. a	13. d	14. d	15. d	16. b	17. b	18. d	19. d	20. d
21. a	22. b	23. b	24. b	25. a	26. c	27. b			

Chapter 25
1. d	2. c	3. a	4. d	5. d	6. d	7. d	8. d	9. d	10. a
11. c	12. c	13. d	14. b	15. d	16. d	17. c	18. b		

www.ingramcontent.com/pod-product-compliance
Lightning Source LLC
Chambersburg PA
CBHW082205230426
43672CB00015B/2909